WOMEN IN WAITING

Women in Waiting

Prejudice at the Heart of the Church

JULIA OGILVY

B L O O M S B U R Y

LONDON • NEW DELHI • NEW YORK • SYDNEY

A Continuum book

Bloomsbury Publishing Plc
50 Bedford Square
London WC1B 3DP

www.bloomsbury.com

Bloomsbury is a registered trademark of Bloomsbury Publishing Plc

Bloomsbury Publishing, London, New Delhi, New York and Sydney

A CIP record for this book is available from the British Library.

ISBN: 9781472901774

10 9 8 7 6 5 4 3 2 1

Typeset by Fakenham Prepress Solutions, Fakenham, Norfolk NR21 8NN
Printed and bound in Great Britain by CPI Group (UK) Ltd, Croydon,
CR0 4YY

To all the wonderful women in my life – you know who you are

'Our lives begin to end the day we become silent about things that matter'
Martin Luther King

Contents

Acknowledgements   ix

Introduction   1

Chapter 1 The Reverend Lucy Winkett   11
         2 The Venerable Sheila Watson,
            the Archdeacon of Canterbury   27
         3 The Reverend Rose Hudson-Wilkin,
            Chaplain to the Speaker of the
            House of Commons   41
         4 The Reverend Vivienne Faull, Dean of York   57
         5 The Reverend Tamsin Merchant   73
         6 Dr Elaine Storkey   89
         7 Dr Jane Williams   105
         8 The Reverend Professor Sarah Coakley   121
         9 Dr Alison Elliot, OBE   137
        10 The Most Reverend Dr Katharine
            Jefferts Schori, Presiding Bishop   151
        11 The Right Reverend Chilton Knudsen,
            Assistant Bishop of New York   167
        12 Helena Kennedy, Baroness Kennedy
            of the Shaws, QC   185

Glossary   199
About the Author   203
Note from the Author   204
List of Illustrations   205

Acknowledgements

This book would not exist without the remarkable women who agreed to tell their stories. I am so grateful for their courage and their contributions, and glad that I was lucky enough to have so much time with them. I am certain they will inspire many young women to follow their calling into the Church.

The advice and support of my godfather, Bishop Michael Turnbull, has been invaluable. He put up with endless technical questions and provided wise advice on many occasions. He was one of a number of Church leaders and friends both here and in America who took the time to help me find my interviewees. I am also indebted to the Rochester Report for helping me to clarify the arguments in the introduction.

I am tremendously lucky to have been part of some special churches in my life including Kilconquhar Church, Holy Trinity Church in St Andrews, 'Sconset Chapel in Nantucket and now Cornerstone St Andrews. The women in my prayer group – Fiona, Bridie, Charlotte, Tamara and Sarah – inspire me every day and the Stirling family teach us all so much about living a Christian life in the real world with all the challenges and frustrations along the way. My fellow pilgrims to Medjugorje and the members of the Monday groups at Hepburn Gardens have also taught me so much. I so appreciate the wise counsel and support of friends like Fi Hughes D'Aeth, Colette Douglas-Home, Judy Holding, Bruce Rigdon, Carol Kinsley, Stephanie Heald, Jerram Barrs, Mark and Jenny Stirling, Sarah Robinson, Stephanie and Wes Vander Lugt, Sarah Brown, Graham McLean, Heather Armstrong, the Lord family, the great women of 'Sconset, our friends in Rwanda and so many others. They are always immensely gracious even if they don't always agree with my arguments. I am also very grateful to the inspiring team at Tearfund, particularly Matthew, Clive, Andrew and all my fellow trustees, who demonstrate such generosity of spirit and service to others.

My thanks to my wonderful agent Maggie Pearlstine and to my charming editor Robin Baird-Smith at Bloomsbury for believing in the importance of this book. Also to Joel, Helen, Maria, and all those involved along the way.

Finally, as always, I feel so blessed to have the unwavering support and love of my husband James and our remarkable children Flora and Alexander as well as our extended families.

Introduction

The concept of 'prejudice at the heart of the Church' is controversial but there are few contemporary issues that have caused as much pain to the women involved. Most of the recent arguments about the issue of women bishops in the Church of England or the ordination of women in the Roman Catholic Church make no sense to those who are not religious. If anything they simply deflect people from some of the more important concerns of the Church and the good work that is being done in its name across the world. Although I am a Christian I had managed to let most of this pass me by until I became involved in international development and understood more about the oppression of women. That issue alone makes this book relevant to anyone who cares about the misuse of power in our world today.

As a businesswoman I had not experienced a great deal of prejudice so I was shocked when the Anglican Church voted against women bishops in November 2012. I wanted to know more about the women who were reduced to tears on that day when, according to the Reverend Lucy Winkett, the Church succeeded in 'detonating its credibility with contemporary Britain'. She was right about that if you saw the media storm that followed. In a country that likes to be known for its tolerant attitude, with influence across the world way above its size, seeing this story on international news was a major embarrassment and sent an appalling message to women across the world. I was not surprised to read of the then Archbishop of Canterbury's 'deep personal sadness' after the vote.

Although I had grown up in the Church of England I had moved north and joined the Church of Scotland where women ministers were not uncommon and I couldn't have imagined a situation in 2012 when anyone could possibly be seen to discriminate against one group of people in that way even within a very patriarchal Church setting. Not surprisingly our Prime Minister felt the same, leading to angry exchanges in the media and veiled threats of Parliament stepping in. The Church of England is not some sideshow that can be ignored. It is the established Church, and Her Majesty the Queen is the Supreme Governor, appointing the senior figures on the recommendation of the Prime Minister. Parish priests take an oath of allegiance to the Queen and carry a pastoral responsibility for the whole of their parish and not just their Christian congregation. With 26 Bishops sitting in the House of Lords as 'Lords Spiritual' it is answerable to Parliament and therefore firmly part of the political process.

As I was to discover, it really was a surprise to many that the vote was lost in 2012 and particularly to the women who had worked for years to get this through. The complexity of the Church of England governance means that the three different Houses of Bishops, Clergy and Laity need to approve the decision by a two-thirds majority to consecrate women bishops. Both the House of Bishops and Clergy had agreed but the House of Laity was lost by a few votes. A kind of democracy had prevailed although whether that group can really be said to represent the views of the parishioners is another matter since 42 out of 44 dioceses had voted in favour.

I wanted to know more about the women who had fought so hard against this apparent injustice. As a trustee of Tearfund, a Christian international relief and development charity working with churches across the world to eradicate poverty, I am often faced with the terrible impact of patriarchal systems on women. The horrors of the sex trade, of contemporary slavery and of domestic abuse often stem from the way women are perceived as lesser beings. More girls were killed in the last 50 years for being girls than men in all the wars of the twentieth century. Three million women have been kidnapped or sold to the sex trade. How could the Church of England, leader of the 85 million Anglicans across the world, send any kind of message that women are not of equal worth and should not be properly valued when this is so different to what Jesus tells us in the Bible about love and compassion? Why is the Church not focusing its energy on the real issues that are devastating our society from poverty, domestic abuse and the collapse of the family to our rampant materialism and terrifying levels of anxiety as young people feel they can't live up to society's expectations of them?

The more I discovered about women in the Church, the more I wanted to meet some of them. They tell their stories on these pages and for all the stories of prejudice and intolerance there is always a great sense of hope, love, forgiveness and courage. Being called to be a priest is not just some vain wish for a particular career nurtured since childhood but is something much more intangible, a gift from God that makes all the difficulties they face worthwhile.

For many men and women it is wrong to allow our culture to dictate to the Church but I personally believe that as Christians we have a mission to serve others and to reach out to those who are outside the Church and we need to reflect our culture if we are to do that effectively. Women need to see other women leading and all kinds of diversity can only strengthen human life. My experience in marriage and business is that women and men work very well together and I am equally passionate that women should have an ability to transform organisations like the Church. In 1948 the Declaration of Human Rights rightly affirmed the dignity of the human person and that all human life was sacred, irrespective of gender. For Canon Jane Charman, the Director of Learning for Discipleship and Mission in the Diocese of Salisbury, the debate 'is about nothing less than the identity before God of female human beings as equally valued and equally loved'.

I only have to read my Bible to see how Jesus felt about women. In John 4 he has a remarkable conversation with a Samaritan woman he meets at a well. He asks for some water from her cup. It was an extraordinary moment for him as he did something that no respectable Jewish man of the time would ever have done. Not only was he talking to her alone but she was a woman from a much-hated mixed-race and one who had apparently had five husbands. He speaks to her with love and respect and in this moment he opens up the possibility that there need be no barriers or walls between people. He makes it clear that all of us are deeply loved in the eyes of God and she becomes his first real evangelist, rushing off to tell her town what he has said and done. It is hard to believe that people can read stories like this and still fail to recognise that women can answer the call of God and lead the Church. This is one example among so many and each interviewee has provided both their favourite verse and their most inspiring woman from the Bible. Not surprisingly Mary Magdalene and Martha are mentioned most often, reminding us just how crucial they are to the story of Jesus and of course Mary, the mother of Jesus, is a crucial figure in the Roman Catholic and Eastern Orthodox Churches as well as to many in the Anglican Church.

Women also played a key role in the creation and life of the early Church as theologians, activists, abbesses, nuns, mystics, saints, martyrs and missionaries. They founded many religious institutions and later many schools and hospitals. During the Middle Ages convents became powerful institutions in Europe and had great influence. Well-known examples include St Joan of Arc and St Catherine of Siena who was a theologian and member of the Dominican order but also had a key role as a diplomat and focused on the reform of the clergy. St Teresa of Avila, a Spanish mystic and Carmelite nun was another prominent figure in the Church with her emphasis on the search for inner peace.

However I also understand that there are people with genuinely held beliefs who do not wish to see women as bishops and it is important to mention some of the arguments here. I am indebted to the Rochester Report for providing a useful summary of many of the issues facing the General Synod of the Church of England when they began their crucial debates in 2005.

A key moment for women was the vote in favour of the ordination of women as deacons in 1986 and as priests in 1992. The first 32 woman priests were ordained in March 1994 in Bristol Cathedral and now one-third of all priests and almost half of all ordinands are women, although that number has recently started to decline. The majority of clergy and lay members of the Church agreed with that decision and there are other parts of the

Anglican Communion who had already reached that conclusion as well as other Protestant Churches (the Episcopal Church in America ordained women as priests in 1976). However, there has been a growing number of people who agree with parts of the Anglican Province (such as in parts of Africa) and with the Roman Catholic and Eastern Orthodox Church that this is wrong. The puzzle is why women were ordained as priests but not as bishops as happened in the Episcopal Church in America but it seems to have been a step too far for those against the issue. In particular one of the key roles of a bishop as a focus of unity in the Church has been a stumbling block.

The key arguments in favour of women being ordained as bishops centre on the Bible, tradition, reason and experience. Scripture teaches the essential dignity and equality of women from creation. This equality is disrupted by the Fall, as described in Genesis 3, when sin is brought into the world and life in the Garden of Eden is destroyed but it is then restored in the New Testament as a result of the work of Christ and the gift of the Holy Spirit. Women play a key role in Jesus' life and ministry and women leaders are mentioned in the early Church. Mary Magdalene has been described by many as the first apostle when she tells others that Jesus has risen from the dead. As Nicky Gumbel, Vicar of Holy Trinity Brompton, wrote, 'it was especially amazing that Jesus appeared to her as a woman's testimony would have been considered less weighty'. This and many other moments in his life challenge contemporary views of the role of women.

Women are also involved in a variety of leadership roles in the early Church. The issue of 'headship' was not meant to refer to the patriarchal kind of leadership that we so often see now but to a different kind of mutual submission. Paul's writings on women are at times confusing and some academic theologians would even argue controversially that they are not all the work of one man. In Galatians 3.28 Paul clearly refers to the equality of women ('There is no longer Jew or Greek... there is no longer male and female; for all of you are one in Christ Jesus'.) but in Corinthians he puts everyone back in the social order of the day. Christian tradition is seen as dynamic and developing under the power of the Holy Spirit so ordaining women can be part of a new tradition. Reason and experience show the positive role of women in the Church of England and women have clearly had a genuine calling to ordination. For many, proclaiming the gospel in today's society lacks credibility if women are not properly valued and allowed to use their gifts for leadership. The situation is fundamentally unjust.

The arguments against allowing women bishops are in similar categories. The key issue is the supremacy of God's word in the Bible which cannot necessarily be fitted into our own world view. While Genesis asserts that men and women are equal they have complementary but different roles and we still live in a fallen world. Jesus only called male apostles and never questioned the patriarchy of the Old Testament. The writings of Paul appear to affirm the idea of female subordination. Teaching is led by male priests and the overall leadership is always male. The understanding of 'headship' is a crucial issue as well as the positive aspects of 'servant leadership'. According to tradition the evidence for female leadership in the early Church is unconvincing. Overall leadership by bishops has been a male preserve and there is the issue of apostolic succession. The ordination of women was supposed to be subject to a period of 'reception' which is seen to be incomplete and since the whole Church does not accept women it cannot be seen as the will of God. According to reason it would be wrong to change tradition to suit society and it would be wrong to create the kind of disunity that will follow ordaining women as bishops and the loss of important ecumenical relationships.

Another increasingly significant part of the debate was the potential to have women appointed as bishops on different terms from men. This would have allowed those who couldn't accept their ministry to have alternative oversight from a male bishop and would have meant creating legislation to undermine the authority of female bishops. Parishes have been allowed by law to choose a 'flying bishop' who did not support the ordination of women priests. Some thought that these restrictions would at least allow the vote to go through but for many women this kind of discrimination was impossible and unjust both in law and the eyes of God. This compromise was seen as a theological muddle and felt to be a factor in the failure of the vote in 2012.

These were the kind of arguments that faced the Synod and that still face the Church now. It is hard to know if biblical scholars will ever reach consensus or whether the Church of England can continue to be part of political life if it does not change. The previous Archbishop of Canterbury, Rowan Williams, was clearly devastated by the decision but also in a no-win situation as he tried to preserve some kind of unity at great cost to his own legacy. As I write, a great deal of progress has been made and it is clear that the appointment of Justin Welby as the new Archbishop of Canterbury has been fairly crucial to this. The Church in Wales voted for women bishops in September 2013 and Anglicans in Ireland have appointed their first female bishop. The Scottish Episcopal Church agreed on women bishops in 2003 but has yet to appoint one. In England the General Synod met in November 2013 and approved a package of measures as the next steps to enable women to become bishops. There will be further consultation but a final vote is likely to be taken later in 2014. Meanwhile eight women have recently been allowed to attend and speak but not vote in the House of Bishops. More conservative groups like Forward in Faith and Reform representing Anglo-Catholics and some conservative Evangelicals may have difficult decisions to make, about staying within the Church of England but in reality their combined membership is only a relatively small percentage of about 1.7 million regular Churchgoers. We may also hope that a Church that feels more relevant will see a great renewal and benefit from the gifts of many talented women. Women have a natural ability to collaborate and a sense of compassion which is sorely needed.

I have also chosen to include the stories of two prominent American women in the Episcopal Church, the Presiding Bishop Katharine Jefferts Schori and the recently retired Bishop of Maine Chilton Knudsen, now Assistant Bishop in New York. The complexities of the situation in America will be described in their chapters but there is no doubt that the impact of decisions across the Atlantic have been felt in England. They don't have the same connection between Church and state but their battles were linked closely to the Civil Rights movement. The ordination of women was finally forced upon the authorities by

a non-violent protest known as the 1974 Philadelphia ordinations, more typical of other activists. Since then the ordination
of the first openly gay Bishop Gene Robinson created even more
headaches for the Archbishop of Canterbury, Rowan Williams,
as he tried to retain unity across an increasingly divided
Anglican Communion. I have also interviewed a prominent
Catholic, Helena Kennedy QC and the first female Moderator
of the Church of Scotland, to reflect a view of women in other
key Christian Churches.

I am not going to apologise for the strong wording of the title
of this book or for failing to interview women who are against
the appointment of women bishops. I originally thought I might
do so but it became clear to me that I simply could not accept
or perhaps even respect their arguments. I am not an academic
theologian but I am a Christian called to love my neighbour,
whoever that might be. In my work in the non-profit world
it is obvious to me what kind of damage is done when people
judge others simply for their sex or race. People can sit around
in the Synod discussing complex theological arguments but this
book demonstrates the reality of life for women who answer
their calling to the Church and on occasions go through great
personal suffering.

While researching the book I talked to many other young
women who have a sense of calling to leadership in the Church
but feel it is wrong to follow that path. They have no sense
of affirmation and suffer the pain of denying that call. I don't
believe this is the kind of self-sacrifice that we are called to as
Christians. Sheryl Sandberg's recent best-selling book 'Lean
In: Women, Work and the Will to Lead' calls on women to
Lean In to improve their career opportunities, but that must
be so difficult in such a patriarchal world as the Church which
reinforces patterns that consistently diminish women. So often
women apologise for having a passion for something or for
sounding too ambitious when that would be so normal for a
man in the same situation. For those women that have had the
courage to pursue their calling they often feel that they have to
do everything five times better than a man.

Most of my interviewees have that sense of being watched
and judged because they are a woman in a more typically

man's world. They suffer from a casual prejudice that leads to comments on their hair, weight or clothing in a way that rarely happens to men. In their experience it is personal encounters with women in the Church that change long-held views based on prejudice rather than sound theological arguments. Perhaps personal encounters with women in this book will help to change views and open minds to the incredible potential we have in the Church and ensure women are no longer kept waiting.

1

The Reverend Lucy Winkett

If you have followed the story of the ordination of women over the last 20 years or you are a regular listener to Radio 4's *Thought for the Day* you are likely to be familiar with Lucy Winkett. Described by the Bishop of London in 2010 as 'among the most talented priests in her generation' and by Ruth Gledhill of *The Times* on Radio 4 as one of our 'most-loved women priests' she has suffered more than her fair share of pain as she has followed her calling to serve God. For anyone outside the Church and used to a world of employment tribunals when things go wrong, her stoicism in the face of the adversity she has suffered both from the press and from male clergy opposed to women's ordination may seem hard to understand. She has been outspoken in her frustration at the Synod's failure to vote for women bishops in 2012 and in the process 'detonating its credibility with contemporary Britain' but as she says, 'we will hang on by our fingertips, sad and furious in equal measure, until the authority of women and men is accepted by the Church we love but, at times like this, find impossible to defend' (*Guardian* 20/11/2012).

Lucy was well known in the early years of the ordination of women for her role as a canon at St Paul's Cathedral but she is now vicar of the seventeenth-century Church of St James's Piccadilly. Anyone who works in the area around Jermyn Street in central London will know the beautiful building designed by Christopher Wren that sits at the heart of the community, not far from the tempting shop windows of Fortnum and Mason. It is known for the busy daily market in the front courtyard, its impressive range of concerts and for the number of homeless people who gather there, knowing they are welcome to sleep peacefully in the pews throughout the day. Somehow this typifies Lucy's approach to the Church: her love of music and peaceful contemplation and yet her willingness to fight for issues of social justice and to live and work on one of the noisiest streets in London.

When you first meet Lucy you are immediately struck by her gentleness and the warmth of her smile, whilst also sensing a tougher side to her beneath the surface. We sat together in the tidy but cosy study of her Georgian rectory on Piccadilly, once she had managed to dry off her rain-drenched dog. She is in her mid-40s but seems younger and was dressed simply in a clerical black shirt and dog collar with a purple skirt. I could imagine sharing just about anything with her and wonder how anyone could have been as unkind as they were to her in her early days at St Paul's Cathedral. Her life is exceptionally busy, with a number of roles alongside her life as a vicar including chairing the governors of a new academy school; being a founding advisor of the theological think tank Theos; speaking and writing on culture, gender and religion; leading retreats, and playing in pubs with a band called 'The Smiling Strangers'. Although Lucy studied history at Cambridge, her initial career choice was music. She has a stunning soprano voice and auditioned successfully for the Royal College of Music but she explains that before she got there she had 'a quietly dramatic' change of direction towards the Church.

'When I left university I had visions of being a singer but between getting the audition to go to the Royal College of Music and actually going I completely changed direction, although I did end up doing the training for a year. My calling was quite quietly dramatic ... no angel arrived and there were no choruses. It was in one moment really. I was visiting my parents in Buckinghamshire and wasn't really going to church much at the time. I'd grown up in the Church and I'd been in the church choir but I was off it so I went to evensong really to have an hour to myself. The vicar there was talking about the appearance of success and it was something to do with that phrase, although I still don't really know what it means. The interpretation I put on it later was that I had visions of myself being a singer and that to be a successful singer you need to be on stages and it's quite obvious what success looks like as a singer. And I think I imagined that and all that I did in that moment was to walk away from that success. And it suddenly felt, in a way that it hadn't done before, less meaningful, more empty for me.

'And I thought to myself, "Oh my goodness I'm going to be a priest." And that was really exciting, shocking, disorientating. I felt energetic about it but I just sat quietly in the pew. It was such a boring service as well, that's the interesting thing about it, it wasn't very emotive, it was very quiet. But I was really sure, a click like a round peg fitting in a round hole. And I thought, "What am I going to do? I don't quite know how to do this." I'd never seen a woman in a dog collar. This was before women could be priests and I didn't connect myself with the people up at the front at all because they were all men. I grew up in a church that was quite High Church and I remember saying that I'd quite like to join the servers team and the head server, who was a lovely man, said he would not allow 'serviettes' in his sanctuary. So that was it and I just accepted it. I was a girl; girls didn't do that kind of thing.

'I went back to see my parents that Sunday night and I thought "I'm not going to tell anybody yet because it's so exciting" and I didn't know what to do about it. So the first person I told was the managing director of the market research company where I was working, demonstrating photocopiers, and he was terrified and said, "All right, calm down love, alright, alright." And that was my first time getting it out there. You just think, "If I say this out loud, this might make it real and people might laugh and they might not get it." And it's so precious you don't really want to say it. I did tell my family and friends gradually because I had to decide what to do. I went to see the vicar and talked to him a little bit. He is retired now and he's a very lovely person but opposed to the ordination of women, so that was a bit of a tough conversation. He sent me on to a woman deacon to talk about it and she was very encouraging.

'I'd had a very acute experience of bereavement which I was coming out of, which is why I think she was slightly cautious at first. She wanted to make sure that I wasn't making a dramatic choice in the wrong direction. So she did kind of slow me down a bit, which was right. His name was Andrew. He fell while climbing in the Chamonix Valley and was in a coma for ten days and then he died. So it was very, very difficult. We were both 22 and you just think that the future is going to be something and then it isn't. I resisted any connection at the time with my change of plan and maybe when I'm very old I'll look back and see connections that I don't see now. But I think that the process of grief is very messy and doesn't make any sense. So I resist making sense of it by then saying, "I did this because of that."

'So I saw the Deacon and then you get put into this sausage machine and you have to go through interviews and you have to apply. You get sent to various different people and asked your life story and they need to discern with you whether they think you have a calling and after three days at a residential they either recommend you or they don't. But for the women in that group we were being selected to be deacons. And then there was this rather odd moment where I was asked, "If it ever became possible for women to be priests would you consider being a priest?" And I said, "Absolutely, I don't feel called to be a deacon, I feel called to be a priest but I understand that that's not possible so I shall be content to do what I'm permitted to do." But I always felt in my heart that it was definitely the priesthood for me. I started training at Queen's College in Birmingham and it was during my training to be a deacon that the vote happened. I did my curacy in Manor Park in east London and it was brilliant training. I had a great vicar who was very community-minded. He would send me to community meetings on the estate and I would do home communions and three or four funerals a week, which was very good grounding. You're slightly thrown in at the deep end and you just have to get on with it. As a woman I had some moments, such as funerals, where the family would turn up and say, "She's not taking our Alf's funeral, get her out" and that kind of thing.

'Then I went to St Paul's Cathedral as a minor canon and chaplain in 1997, having been ordained as a priest in 1995. St Paul's hadn't appointed a woman in any capacity there before but I think the new Dean rightly thought, "If this person is the best candidate then we must appoint her." I went through the very straightforward appointments process with an interview and singing audition because you do a lot of singing as a minor canon. It was important, particularly because of the events that followed that I'd been through that process. I needed to be able to say that I was the best candidate and I hadn't just been appointed because I was a woman, because there was a lot of nastiness.

'There are eight clergy at St Paul's including three minor canons. They are a little team by themselves and do all the daily services including communion, the singing and organising all the special services. I was one of these junior posts. The Dean and Chapter appoint you but two of them didn't really want this appointment. I believe them when they say it wasn't because of me and because I wasn't good enough in some way. They just didn't want the divisiveness. And one of them in particular, who became a friend of mine and has now died, was really clear that it was bringing division into the heart of the Cathedral. He was very, very angry.

'I don't know how the story broke in the *Evening Standard* but it did the day after I was appointed. I was away skiing and my mum phoned me up in tears and said, "You're on the front page of all the national newspapers." And I couldn't think why. I didn't know where they'd got pictures from. It was seven months before I actually started so it was seven months of dread with the press, it was horrid. They got hold of Andrew's picture somehow and put that story all over one Sunday paper. I couldn't believe the way the press operated. I was really shocked. I had no idea that they make stuff up, so that was a very searing experience.

'I had a long conversation with the Dean, wondering if I should change my mind as I didn't know if I could take it. There was one journalist who has since died but who just kept the story going, writing articles every month or so. Little articles, "So and so has resigned, the bell ringers are in uproar, they are awaiting the new woman." There was a guy who took the Dean and Chapter to Court because the statutes all say "he" and he was made a vexatious litigant in the end. It just went on and on and on and you think, "I should just stay here in my box". The press were camped outside my flat and I had to go straight into a press conference at St Paul's on my first day to explain why I was dividing the Church of England. There was also a TV crew making a fly-on-the-wall documentary for 18 months about St Paul's, which happened to coincide with my arrival. So while all the horrible stuff was happening I was trying hard to do a new job and be the first woman without making a big deal of that and being followed around all the time by these cameras.

'Looking back, I just got on with it. I wasn't really complaining but for at least two years it was very hard. I've got really good friends so that's helpful but the times that I remember it being very hard were actually in public. I would be celebrating the Eucharist under the dome at St Paul's with lots of people around and normally I would hold my arms up but there was a period of some weeks where I couldn't do this. I was shaking and I just didn't quite have the strength to do it. So I used to rest my hands on the altar, because I had to sing as well and it was impossible to ignore the fact that I was female when I was singing. I can sing so it was a strong sound and I wanted it to envelop the atmosphere. I was proud to be a woman singing there but I just couldn't lift my arms. It was a very strong physical reaction. I think looking back now it was bewildering and disorientating and I often felt terrible. I probably had a few panic attacks.

'It did take its toll. But at the time I just didn't take account of that very much because I thought that it was important that I was doing what I was doing. What I kept in mind was, "I'm just doing my job." My predominant prayer to God was, "What's happening? Please could you help me because I don't understand why this is so hard and I don't know why these people are being so horrible?" There was some really bad behaviour although we are all reconciled now.

'There was one particular canon who was the one who was very angry about my appointment. He never received communion from me and would always walk out every time I walked into the Chapel if he realised I would be taking communion. He would not be present when I celebrated, which was hard for me. I think it was probably hard for him too. He was very, very committed to reconciliation with the Roman Catholic Church as he saw it, so his was the ecumenical argument that ordaining women brought unity with Rome very much further away. We were in the press a lot together and I felt sorry for him because he got couched as a kind of old misogynist, with me as this bright young thing, getting the sympathy. We got on really well actually but then he got very ill towards the end of my time there. He retired and died very shortly after his retirement. And there's a rather lovely story about this and I hope his widow doesn't mind me telling it. When I became a canon I moved into his house. There was a knock at the door one day and his wife turned up with an urn of his ashes and she said, "I'm sure he would like you to be the person to look after these." So we went to the Cathedral and put them on the altar and I said prayers and he stayed there overnight and was buried the next day. And he'd said that he would like me to take part in his memorial service when he knew he was dying. So there was a very amazing reconciliation that happened there.

'This experience definitely made me stronger as a person. I think I've got a mixture of a kind of breeziness which is, "Get on with it", and also I know how to dig deep. And that's digging deep into spiritual resources, into God, it's not me. I couldn't have done that. That's why my arms kept collapsing or why I found it hard to walk up the pulpit stairs and preach. It was just so hard and it's such a public place as well. You're always doing everything in front of a thousand people. I don't want to be too emotive about this but if I'm talking about how it felt, it felt a little bit like being a butterfly, pinned for everyone to look at and say, "Oh that's our woman priest and doesn't she sing well." And, "Gosh isn't that amazing, isn't that lovely." And then, inside, as was shown by the documentary, the institution was struggling with this new person. I don't know what conclusions I draw from it, except it's a rather clichéd thing to say, "What doesn't kill you makes you stronger." But that's really true.

'Each day I got up and got on with the next day and the people who were struggling with the fact that I was there are not bad people. There's another very amazing story of one of the servers, Ron, who was incandescent that I was there, and he started this thing of the servers all coming up and then refusing communion. You'd go to somebody saying, "The body of Christ", and they would just turn away. It was absolutely horrible and all done very publicly. But after five years of me being there and getting on quite well personally, something happened. It was communion one Sunday morning, with hundreds of people milling about and everyone there under the dome. And I go along the row and I'm just about to miss out Ron. And I see these little tremulous hands held out like this so I just ... I was completely overwhelmed as was he. I said 'The body of Christ', gave him bread and he ate it. And I couldn't get through the service really. It was just a miracle. And then after the service he was helping me take my coat off as we wear these bejewelled, blingy coats and I said, "Ron, Ron, what was that?" And he said, "Just remember, Lucy, there's no fool like an old fool."' Amazing. So I gave him a hug. And we were fine from then on but it took him five years.

'Part of the difficulty about talking about the really tough times is that, one by one, we were all reconciled, even with the Canon in death. I bear absolutely no ill will, I really mean that. And I didn't win anything, I didn't triumph, I hate all that language. I think it's wrong but together, somehow, we got through it. That's probably why in the end there was this odd decision for me as a minor canon to become a canon straight away which has never happened in the whole of St Paul's history. After six years I was wondering what I might do next, when I got a letter from Downing Street asking me to be the Precentor Canon at St Paul's Cathedral. I was quite keen on leaving and doing something else as you can imagine but it was the job of precentor which is the musical and liturgical job and St Paul's is an extraordinary place. It's an amazing place to be able to find a liturgical language that invites people into the presence of God. It meant that in the end I was able to leave well, reconciled and with a joyful feeling after such a tough start.'

As Lucy finished talking about her experience at St Paul's I felt very moved by her courage and her ability to retain a sense of perspective about such a challenging experience. I was particularly affected by the extraordinary mental and physical struggle she went through just to lead the sacrament of communion. She clearly needed her sense of humour and she veered from laughter to tears as she described just a few of the incidents that happened there. A friend once said that she had even been spat on by some members of the clergy who had chosen to sit at the back as she processed up the aisle, something that I would have found almost impossible to forgive. I imagined there must have been a slight sense of relief to move to the very different environment of St James's Piccadilly.

'Coming to St James's Piccadilly was very different, even though it's very close in some ways. I wanted to be in a parish. In a cathedral you have a big job with big budgets and it is high profile but I love the reputation of this church which does very different things and has a strong tradition of being liberal theologically and of social engagement. The word that I think the church would like to use about itself is "progressive". I love that. I love trying to think and it pushes me.

'I think what I'm passionate about is that the Christian faith is an irresistible invitation. I'm not forced into something, I'm invited into it but it's so compelling that I can't take my eyes off it. We don't seem to be terribly good in the Church at explaining that or living it, or showing it in some way. So where I love to be, my favourite type of place to be is not necessarily in a church setting. We do an annual service with the Royal Academy. We have the church packed full of artists, most of whom think the Church is a total waste of time, that it's passé, its confining, its inhibiting of their freedom of spirit and speech and all the rest of it. I love being in that mix and saying, "Have you ever seen Christianity really as I think you could?" Because I think it's extraordinary. And it sets you free and it's not about confining you. So all of St James's reputation was about that. And there's a very dedicated parish community here with people travelling in from all over London.

'We have an amazing footfall too. People just walk through the church all the time, lots of homeless people and people who are quite literally lost. I see Piccadilly Circus as a really profound metaphor for people who are running around in circles. We've got all the hedge fund guys in Jermyn Street who are working every hour God sends and are exhausted all the time. They have pizza brought to their desks and they have their shirts taken away and the doctor comes to look at them and they don't even ever have to leave the office. And then we've got a whole bunch of other people who have absolutely nothing to do and nowhere to be who sleep in the pews. But I think that's an amazing contrast.

'And I think there is a theological link between beauty and justice. At St James's there's a really amazing opportunity to explore that and it is part of the reason we want to restore our church. It has the most stunning history and it's a light, beautiful building. Part of the reason we want to restore and redecorate and reinvigorate the church building is so that homeless people can sleep in it. It's not the only reason but I believe that something permeates out from beautiful surroundings that people have made to the glory of God. There is a message that gives. And that's why we not only "allow" people but we welcome people to sleep in the pews. And if a guy in a suit came in and wanted to sleep in the pews he'd be very welcome too.

'In my book *Our Sound is our Wound* the theme that underpins it is my belief that our "faster is better than slower, louder is better than quieter" society is an expression of our fear of silence, which in turn is a foretaste of our fear of the great silence – death. We are like a primitive society gathered in a clearing in the woods banging things together frantically to keep away the imagined beasts in the dark. We are afraid of darkness and silence and we make everything noisy and light. I live here near Piccadilly Circus and it's just 24/7 chaos. It drives me crazy because I am very sensitive to noise and I'm just fascinated by what we have done to ourselves as a human race. People are living chaotic lives whether they are in or out of work. And what interests me is that sometimes I imagine this whole area as it must have been in 1684, all green fields. How have we got here? Why have we made things like this? Because we have collectively chosen this somehow. And what does this say about how we want to live or who we want to be as human beings. Efficiency has become a bit of an idol and a bit of a god.

'I'd also say that individually and collectively our voice can set us free. That probably goes back to my experience at St Paul's in my singing role. I sang at the altar and was unavoidably female and singing at a different register and I found that very thrilling and invigorating. And at the times when the institution was at its worst I couldn't sing. I lost my confidence and I had to go and practise a lot more. It was only when I dug deep and rooted myself again that I thought I could sing again. But that's not just as an individual, I think that's a collective thing. I'm really happy and energised in the task of helping my parishioners to find their voice as individuals and in this parish.'

Lucy has found various ways to deal with the 'noise' in her life including taking holidays to very remote places but I was interested in how she manages to get any kind of balance in her life between the complexities of her role and finding time for prayer and reflection. I was not sure whether she would really want to encourage other young women to take on such a challenge.

'Being a vicar is a stressful and demanding job. I have a collaborative style but not so collaborative that I don't make decisions. I have become much more competent, chairing meetings, getting through my admin and speaking in public as well as taking services. But I know this set of competencies become very brittle and hollow unless I keep praying and I'm a servant as well. That's very important although hard if I have a deficit to address or a redundancy among our 18 staff here. I am involved in a training course for women clergy, which is about strategic planning and budgets but is always suffused with theological reflection and prayer.

'When it comes to women in the Church or in Parliament or business they really have to stay alive as women. After a period of historic exclusion there's a period of gratitude where women are expected simply to kind of knuckle down and join in. It's really important to keep that femininity or whatever it is that you're bringing that is different. I was in a campaign meeting recently where there were women priests and lay women as well as some men. I found it very moving when one of the women stood up and said, "I've been campaigning for the ordination of women for 30 years. I have stuffed envelopes, I've licked stamps, I was outside Church House. And I don't know why I bothered because the Church hasn't changed, you women priests have not changed the Church." And I think that's a very important conversation for us to have. People in the pews are hoping that women priests will do it differently but it is hard. Women priests have only been ordained for almost 20 years. And there's a Catch 22 in there. There was all this energy and the sense that the new world has begun but how different is the Church now. At the same time, don't blame the women. It was a false expectation to hope that this rather small number of women would get into that layer of the church hierarchy, into the decision-making structures and instantly change it. With my experience at St Paul's, as one amongst all of the men, it's very hard to effect proper change. You become totemic and you can, if you're not careful, start to be a kind of shoring-up mechanism. "Oh, we've got one of those now so we don't need to do anything else." You start to shore up an unjust structure.

'So all women have to ask themselves, "Where am I in those unjust structures? What am I perpetuating? And am I challenging some of the assumptions that are there?" And to keep that energy up is hard but it is vital if the Church really is going to change.

'I think that having women and men in the room does change the agenda and changes the atmosphere of a meeting. And to have an all-male group running a religious institution is just weird. I understand all of the historic reasons but men will often say that as soon as women are there they'll start to talk a little bit more openly or they'll tell different stories or different decisions are made. So I do believe in that change but I don't want to set up women as the saviours of the Church. It's undoubtedly true that if people come to the church here and they see a woman celebrating the Eucharist, it has a different effect from seeing a man celebrate. And it's still new enough, quite often, for people to find a different language in that and a different freedom.

'I would definitely recommend women to come into the Church in spite of all the stress I have had. I said this to a cab driver the other day, when he was looking at my collar and laughing. And he said, "Oh, do you like it?" and I replied, "It is, quite honestly, the best job in the world." It's amazing and I wouldn't be doing it if I didn't think that. I feel very happy doing it, at the same time as it's a real challenge of course.

'I am obviously very pro-women bishops and what I really think is that the Gospel of Jesus Christ is very radical about women. And the Church in its first two centuries gave in to society's expectations of what men and women did, and particularly with respect to the Roman household codes. Right at the very beginning the Church followed society in an unhelpful way and since then the Church has just been missing a really essential component of its leadership. We should have ordained women as deacon, priest and bishop all in one go. "You either have women or you don't. Either you ordain us or you don't baptise us. The sacraments are not for the Church to control." That's a quote from June Osborne [Dean of Salisbury], in the debate of 1992. It has felt so grudging, deacons in 1986, priests in 1992, maybe bishops soon. I do have very good friends who are opposed to the ordination of women and I want to keep those relationships going but ultimately I think the Church has to decide "yes" very simply and not put in place all these complicated arrangements. If one of my colleagues then says to me, "You're pushing me out of the Church", my response would be, "I'm not pushing you out of the Church, I think this is the way the Church has to go for the good of the Church. You make your decision in relation to that."

'There is a general issue about confidence in the Church. Most of the people who walk past or even come into this church are not only indifferent towards the Church but they're actively hostile. They're fed up with the Church arguing about women and sexuality, and they want the Church to talk about things like the gap between the rich and the poor. The central message of the Church is love and compassion, that's got to be where it starts and ends. It's about how the Church shows love and compassion to the people who do not belong to it.

'The Church does have to make friends with the media and I suppose I'd come back to the word "confidence" because I would stand Christianity alongside any other philosophy, any other world religion, and have confidence in its own ability to have something to say. There's a kind of diffidence about Anglicanism which serves us well a lot of the time but this diffidence can really put concrete boots on us at times, so that we're worried about saying things about love and compassion. And I also think that to live a Christian life is hard. It's really hard because it's about forgiveness and it's about love and suffering with other people. It's self-emptying. And I think we live in an age where we're so hung up on our identity, who we are in comparison with other people and so competitive with each other that that way of living is incomprehensible. The difficulty is that it's easy to describe the problem but not to describe the solution and we're not living that as a Church. We need to live it. It's about a kind of redeemed, dignified humility, where you know who you are and you give that person for the life of the people who you don't know. I try my hardest but I don't manage to do it because it's hard.

'I've been talking with some people recently in their 30s in a mix of professions. They are really interested in Christianity but they don't want a kind of wishy-washy, anything-goes Christianity. They want something which is going to change the way they live. And for liberal Christianity, which is what we are, we've often gone too far down that road that whatever you think is fine when it really isn't. There's a fear of clericalism, of vicars shouting down from pulpits, threatening that you're going to go to hell if you don't do this. We don't do any of that here but there is a really demanding commandment from Christ that you should love God and your neighbour as yourself. It's as simple as that.'

As I left Lucy's office I felt incredibly energised and moved by her enthusiasm for the Church and her trust in God throughout all the pain she has suffered. It has given her a tremendous strength and wisdom which she can rely on for the rest of her life and an ability to genuinely share the challenges and pain that others face every day, from the hedge-fund manager to the homeless person. Tears welled up as she described the moment Ron held out his hands for communion and I imagine that kind of emotional response will never leave her but it makes her both human and somehow seem closer to God. I was struck by the gift she has been given of modelling both patience and love in an extraordinary way. Lucy has continued to 'love her neighbour' in circumstances that many of us would find hard to imagine. She is too humble to appreciate any mention of a future for her as a bishop or even an archbishop but I can't help thinking she is just the person to transform the Anglican Church.

Favourite verse: Psalm 46.10 'Be still and know that I am God.'

Favourite woman: Martha. She gets a bad press – usually when they think of her they think of washing-up rotas and busyness but she's practical, emotional and not afraid to be angry with Jesus for staying where he is for two days before coming to see Lazarus who is ill. She is also a theologian in the sense that she confesses Jesus as the Messiah in a straightforward way. She is a whole person with different aspects to her character and combines emotion with practicality and spirituality.

2

The Venerable Sheila Watson, the Archdeacon of Canterbury

Stepping into the world of Sheila Watson is like arriving in another country and an altogether different place from Lucy Winkett's (Chapter 1) life near Piccadilly Circus. Leaving the hustle and bustle of the town of Canterbury behind, you walk into the Cathedral Close and enter into another world that feels calm, peaceful and almost mystical. As you cross the garden behind her house, once a chamber for guests to the monastery, you step over the ruins of the ancient monastic buildings and open a heavy black door into the fifteenth-century Great Cloister. On a dark winter evening you can hear the sounds of Evensong and imagine yourself surrounded by the ghosts of Benedictine monks and pilgrims.

On this particular day there was a palpable sense of excitement in the air in the Cathedral itself as it was only two days before the enthronement of the new Archbishop of Canterbury, Justin Welby. Volunteers were climbing ladders to arrange flowers, moving furniture and polishing the magnificent collection of silver, whilst film crews set up cameras and lighting. Sheila seemed remarkably calm as she guided me around her favourite places in this beautiful building. First the Chapel of Saints and Martyrs of Our Time behind the ancient stone throne of Augustine to remind us of the real and ever present suffering of those persecuted for their religion. Then the Chapel of St Anselm with its dramatic dark marble altar to reflect the majesty of the mountains of Aosta, Anselm's birthplace in Italy. On past the spot where St Thomas Becket was murdered in 1170 and into the crypt to find Anthony Gormley's dramatic hollow figure created entirely of nails hanging above our heads, forcing us to face the pain of the Passion and Crucifixion. The Cathedral is a place where history really comes alive and allows you to feel the spirit of the past around every corner.

I was a little nervous to be meeting the first female Archdeacon of Canterbury. The title alone sounds intimidating and having heard Sheila's powerful voice from a recorded sermon I visualised her as one of my more formidable schoolteachers mixed with a bit of Maggie Smith as the Dowager Countess of Grantham in *Downton Abbey*. Of course I was quite wrong. She is a pretty, petite and immensely warm and likeable woman who looks a decade younger than her 60 years, chic in her slim black trousers and elegant jacket.

Throughout our conversation I sensed a greater acceptance of the way things had been for a woman of her generation in the Church than there would be for younger women like Lucy Winkett. However it appeared from things Sheila said that there had been a gradual realisation in later years that that this acceptance was wrong. As we began to talk in her elegant sitting room overlooking the Close I asked her about her childhood and her calling to the Church.

'I grew up in Ayrshire with a Church of Scotland background. I have clear memories of going to church with my grandmother but it wasn't an enormous part of life and I can't pretend I was particularly drawn to it. I spent all my free time figure skating. It was when I went to St Andrews University to read classics that something happened. I think a combination of things affected me. My father had been very ill and I was fairly disoriented when I arrived at St Andrews because of course it's a shock when suddenly you're somewhere quite different and I had also given up the figure skating which added to a feeling of uncertainty. I remember going into All Saints Episcopal Church in St Andrews with some friends. Memory plays tricks but I happened to go to the Church when it was focusing on Lent and the whole question of the cross. There was the drama of the liturgy and the vigil and the writings of the Roman Catholic monk Thomas Merton and I just got drawn in. It didn't solve everything but it helped me make sense of things.

'I didn't have a specific religious experience but in faith terms the suffering of God has always seemed to me to be the key to why Christianity makes sense and why I can talk about my faith to other people. I could link it at a personal level with my own worries and say that there isn't a place where God is not, even if it doesn't feel like it. It's saying that you're not on your own with your suffering. It's always seemed to me that if someone's suffering a bereavement or there's been some great tragedy then one can dare to speak about God. I would find it very difficult to do that if it weren't for being able to put it in the context of the suffering God.

'So I began to go to this church and was confirmed there and it was from there that I began to start thinking about doing something in the Church but it was a crazy thought, particularly in the Episcopal Church. I think I just ignored the fact that there weren't women priests. I remember that I was sent around to look at convents which appealed to me in a romantic way but my friend who was a monk always says, "thank God you didn't do that or we'd have spent the next ten years getting you out of it". There just weren't any role models, just one full-time female lay worker in the whole diocese, so no obvious way in for me. However I just kept doing things to see what would happen and I was lucky that the Bishop of St Andrews was enormously supportive. In the end I did some post-graduate theology at Oxford for a year before doing some research at St Andrews, which was really all about me not knowing what to do next.

'Finally things moved on a bit and I ended up with a training plan which included team ministry work in the Episcopal Church in Scotland as the only theological colleges that took women were in England and that would have been expensive for the Church. It would have been more logical to enter the Church of Scotland but it never entered my head. I think it was partly the kind of spirituality that the more Catholic end of the Episcopal Church and the Church of England was about that had spoken to me at some deeper level. Also, there were some female ministers in the Church of Scotland and although they could easily get their first post they then seemed to face many barriers so it wasn't that big a temptation for me. In the Anglican Church we might have a "stained glass" ceiling that's still enshrined in law, unlike in other professions, but there are still similar issues for people to face wherever they are. Making things all right on paper doesn't always solve the actuality.

'After about 18 months I was made a deaconess. There were certain functions I couldn't do but I could do parish work and preaching and after a few years working in Scotland I ended up in a suburban Newcastle parish where loads of people still went to church and there were three services on a Sunday morning. There were baptisms after lunch, there was Evensong, there was the youth group and I loved the educational work helping train leaders who might then lead house groups.

'I felt very grateful to be allowed to do all this and it didn't occur to me to question the fact that I couldn't be a priest. I must have thought that I shouldn't question it too much because if I rock the boat I'll end up out of it. I think at an unconscious level there is that kind of message in a patriarchal organisation and it's not that I think it's intentional but it's about how it has developed. There are subtle ways in which people become quiescent. If you look at the number of women being ordained now, more of them seem to end up in some supporting ministry and I have always wondered how much this is a woman's choice or whether it is an almost unconscious institutional discrimination. I also think there are a lot of women who could be enormously gifted leaders but they don't push so they get neglected. Somebody said to me about another organisation (not the Church) that of course what they're looking for is somebody with a large ego and I thought why? Because even some of the books on leadership would say that it's the quiet person in the corner who turns out to be the person who has turned around a global organisation but there is still this stereotype. It's easy for me to look back and say all that now, but at the time I just think I had enough to cope with, just ploughing on doing what I was doing.

'It's all a great waiting game in a sense, without it being about wasting time, because after I'd been in the north-east I was then offered a job in London. This was a great temptation as I had loved visiting London with my grandparents when I was small and I was very excited by the job. I went to work in what was then called the Education and Community Division of the Diocese of London. It was really appealing for me to be working with parishes and lay leaders. How do you help people to feel confident enough not to ram Christianity down other people's throats but to articulate their faith when it's right to do so? When I got there I saw lots of women in the team, which was really exciting and forward-looking, but how wrong could I have been? London is not a diocese known for its support of women. What I then realised was that this work was marginal work, it was on the fringe, it wasn't for mainstream parishes and that's why it happened to have collected all these women.

'By now I had met my husband Derek and he had a parish in Chelsea. I helped there on Sundays and during this time women were being ordained as deacons which was a big, historic moment. The main change for me when I was ordained as a deaconess in 1987 was being called Reverend and wearing a dog collar but it didn't functionally make a lot of difference otherwise. It was another seven years before the ordination of priests. I think along the way I had finally woken up to the fact that there was something actually wrong here. I had an entirely co-ed education and nobody had ever said that girls can't do exactly the same as boys, so it was a horrible shock when suddenly I couldn't. I also remember when some of the men who'd just come out of college came to start jobs in places I was working and would walk around as if they owned the place. I always felt as though I was there because people were just being kind to me.

'It's always dangerous to generalise but this links with one of the ongoing issues for women which is the confidence issue. I think it is more difficult in largely male institutions and I think it's not always understood because if you try and say anything about it people either think you're asking them to feel sorry for you or that you're criticising them and actually it's neither. Here at Canterbury we're very male. There are two of us women who are part of the chapter residentiary, which is unusual, and we do have a number of women who are vergers but we have a male choir and are very male overall. We had a wonderful conference of about 440 women theologians from all over the world and when some of them were in the cathedral for Evensong they just couldn't believe what it was like. I look at some of the younger women now and what I really give thanks for is that they're fearless, because it wasn't the same in the past. At the same time, I see people in different parts of organisations and think there is still something about women gaining confidence. You can look very confident but inside you're in threads. It can be hard for women to get themselves heard in meetings and in public settings.'

I sensed here that Sheila was opening up on a topic that had become increasingly important to her as she looked back over her life in the Church. At the end of our meeting she said that I shouldn't feel bad if I wanted to leave her out of the book after our conversation and I realised how much the issue of confidence rings true for her personally. It is only as she looks back that she can see how hard it had been to be one of the first women to take such a lead in a male-orientated institution. I had often heard that having just one token woman on a board or in a meeting makes little difference to the atmosphere but once you have a second woman things really start to shift. I had certainly felt that in my business career and was well aware of the effort required to look confident whilst feeling quite the opposite. I wondered about the significance for her of being one of the first women to be ordained as a priest in 1994 in the very public setting of St Paul's Cathedral.

'My ordination was hugely important because I was actually permitted to be the celebrant at the Holy Communion. It was so much at the heart of everything that it's about and it was personal but it was also about taking humanity into all that. It's no longer simply being associated with the male figure. I remember we were all gathered at St Paul's for the service and there was still a court case going on to stop it, led by a priest in London. It was only just before the service that the lawyers solved it all. Then there had been warnings about demos and things but the only demo was some nuns in favour and not just any nuns but Roman Catholics who were pro.

'It was about being part of history. It's not that there's something important in being the first but it was about that sense of something changing at that point. The person who had been trying to bring the court case had been permitted to make an objection during the service. I think he went over his time and some of the male clergy who were there just stood up and started waving their service papers and stopped him. After we'd answered certain questions we had to turn and face the congregation and I just remember there was this huge burst of applause from the whole of St Paul's. It was just amazing that there was this huge affirmation of women doing this, because of course what we'd had a lot of the time was continually having to justify ourselves or we were blamed as the people who were in danger of splitting the Church, in London particularly. I think David Hope, the Bishop of London at the time, had found that very difficult. So again I think that does relate to part of the confidence question as it's not helpful when you're continually faced with being the cause of division. Then the following evening I was the celebrant at the Eucharist for the first time in our parish church at St Luke's Sydney Street in London and I was just bowled over by the number of local people and people from the past who came, and even the Roman Catholic Mayor.

'It still amazes me at any point to preside at the Eucharist and somehow to be that close to what Christ was trying to tell us in that sharing of bread and wine. I think, for those of us who lived through that particular time, it gives us a bit of an insight into what exclusion is about. When you don't have something you don't know what you are missing but you start to get an inkling by standing next to somebody at the altar every time whilst not being allowed to do it. It's not that physically as a woman I couldn't lift the cup or make the sign of the cross, it's actually because you're a woman. I could have taken it if you're really not good enough because you've not passed the right exams, but it's just simply because you're a woman.

'I then had some time out for about four years, working part-time as a freelance consultant and trainer. We'd not been married for long and I wanted a bit of space. We may or may not have had children, so it was that kind of time. I think after about four years I realised I needed to decide what I was going to do next and I kind of fell into a job as one of the selection secretaries at Church House, Westminster, which was the team that ran the residential conferences for those wanting to be ordained. After about a year or so I became the Senior Selection Secretary heading up the team that ran that bit of the process. I loved that job, the bureaucracy drove me mad but we ran about 52 or more residential conferences each year. There was a working party that was looking at the design of the selection conference whilst I was there, the selection criteria, so it was a very creative point to be part of all that. It was very intense because people are at that final stage before they might move to ordination, so it was working with people at an intense point of their vocation.

'I did that job until Derek got appointed in Salisbury and then we faced that problem of juggling two people in the same business. I really wanted to do a parish job but, as the Dean, my husband wasn't allowed to live outside the Close and people wouldn't countenance us having two parishes. I was lucky that I managed to get jobs that sat with what Derek was doing. He's a bit older than me and at 65 he wanted to stop so he was able to follow me when I was offered the role of Archdeacon of Buckingham in 2002. But that's another part of the juggling act. The Church is only just at the beginning of learning what to do with couples when both are ordained.

'I remember being told by one bishop that we shouldn't have two stipends because a stipend was money to live on and his wife had worked for the Church almost full-time for nothing. So I think there's another whole context about how women were perceived. If you have an all-male priesthood and you had a tradition where the wife was going to devote herself to her husband's work unpaid I think it leaves some women feeling disgruntled when there are these women coming along expecting to be ordained and paid.

'I was very torn when the archdeacon role came up at Canterbury in 2007 because I wanted to do a parish at that stage but I felt it was important that some women were doing these jobs and in the end that became the deciding factor. There were only two or three women who were archdeacons at that point so it was significant in that sense. I think the pressure is on then, as with a lot of other contexts, when you're one of the first women to do things. I was more aware of it with something like the archdeacon role where the title doesn't give a clue to people as to what the gender is. I remember going to a dinner and somebody suddenly looking surprised when I appeared by the label because it had never occurred to them I'd be a woman.

They were pleased about it but it could have easily have been the other way. It scared me stiff having this feeling that you've always got to be better than the average or better than the men because you've got to prove not just that it can be done, but that it really is alright for other people. I have found a lot of women resonating with that feeling.

'Thankfully I've worked for the Church for over 30 years now and it's very infrequent that I've ever had people having a go at me as a woman but it is often more invidious than that. I just don't think about it most of the time because I think it's easier to try and get on and do the job so I suppose I may be more conscious of the points at which it's important that there is a woman doing something. For example at the enthronement on Thursday I'll be the first woman to put an Archbishop in the Diocesan Throne and at one level that doesn't matter at all, provided you don't trip or forget your words. It's not as though it's a difficult job but it is important.

'With the debate on women becoming bishops I felt I could contribute something by doing my job and being a symbol. I personally believe that the minute you said women could be priests there was no good reason for them not to be bishops. The only issue is about timing and unity and I disagree with those who put theological arguments against it. There is a question about how everyone lives with each other and I hope we could find a way to work that out. There's undoubted hurt on the way and there are undoubtedly points at which we get it very wrong but what happens with gender questions in the world is highly significant. I'm not someone who's been overseas but when I read the stuff about the difference women's education makes I think you know this question is much bigger than it ever looks. If only people would understand this. It's not about rights.

'The big irony was that I ended up enthroning the Bishop of Chichester, days after the debacle of the debate in 2012 (to consecrate women bishops), when he was one of the three bishops who had voted against women. When I got to Chichester I was amazed because I didn't know what this was going to be like with all the press interest. It just felt slightly weirder than usual and so many people were relieved that I was there because the diocese was not behind the kind of speech that the Bishop had made in the Synod. I think, in a funny kind of way, for the Bishop of Chichester it was important. I mean I've not spoken with him about it but he was saying what he believed and he wasn't out to get anybody in saying that. There was something that was important about saying we are simply the Church getting on with what we need to do. You can probably trace the seam for me which is about a kind of normality even amidst total abnormality. It's somehow somewhere that I've ended up rather than being outspoken.

'When it comes to issues of social justice and the Church speaking out we could do it so much better. My frustration is that I don't think we always engage local Christians with what they do ordinarily or other people with what the Church is doing. I think one of our dangers in terms of our public voice is that we have got bogged down in our own internal affairs. It's hijacked a lot of things, both in the energy it's consumed but also in the way it takes the spotlight off some of the other things that might be being said. I mean things like the "ban the bomb" debate in the General Synod, the role of the Anglican Church in South Africa against apartheid and the whole question of breast milk and Nestlé and all that were very important some years ago. There has been a consistent public voice about social issues but I don't know whether it's because society has changed in terms of the place of the established Church or whether it's about all the internal things that have been going on, such as the women bishops debate, but somehow we don't quite manage to engage at that level in the way that we did. Rowan Williams was tireless in his support for social justice issues and on Christmas Day he would be doing lunch with the homeless. My frustration is that there are huge organisational issues we have had to deal with and in some ways the job I ended up doing wasn't the one I thought I would do.'

As Sheila became more animated about the challenges of women in the Church I was reminded of an article she wrote (in the *Fairacres Chronicle* in 2006) referring to her struggle to find a way to pray amidst the vagaries of her busy life as an archdeacon. She spoke about the need to 'let go', which was something that instantly resonated with me. For many women balancing work, family life and all the other 'voluntary' activities that fill each day, the chance to take time out and, as William Blake put it, 'To see a world in a grain of sand and a heaven in a wild flower' become harder and harder to find. Apparently the average archdeacon spends 63 days per year in a car and as one colleague of hers pointed out, anyone yearning for preferment should know 'how little glamour and how much eating sandwiches in a lay-by' it entailed. Sheila stressed in her article that 'progress in the contemplative life can only be made in proportion to progress in the active life: the two are inextricably bound. It is that compassionate eye of the heart, that mixture of the active and contemplative which so richly offers the chance to banish or get in proportion those silly, wordly frustrations.' I wondered how she could possibly achieve that in her life which is very much lived in the fast lane.

'With difficulty would be the answer to that. On the one hand being in the Cathedral locates me in a rhythm of prayer which means morning and evening prayers every day. If I'm here I'm part of that. Half past seven in the morning is not me at my best, and you will catch me running through the garden to get there by the skin of my teeth. I believe Michael Ramsey (a previous Archbishop of Canterbury) once remarked when somebody asked him how long he'd spent praying that morning, "I spent half an hour trying to and two minutes doing it", which encapsulated something for me. There's a bit of me that rails against the formality but there is something that's important about that horrible word "discipline". I think there's something about people having to find what it is, even if it's once a week or whatever, but what is the thing that's going to help them find the time for prayer or contemplation? I think alongside that there's the exact opposite which is the freedom to allow for your imagination and this depends a lot on your personality. I think imagination as well as silence plays a huge part for me and I think that's true for a lot of women. I love ballet, for example, so I think something like that can be good as it stimulates the imagination but is also about physically moving. I think imagination is about finding things that stimulate you or take you to a different place. It doesn't necessarily leave it all behind, but somehow when you go back to it it's still all there but maybe some tiny perspective has shifted on it.'

Sheila ended that article with some words from St Francis de Sales carved on a Caithness standing stone to mark the Millennium that seemed to sum Sheila up for me as she did her best to honour her calling: 'Do not wish to be anything but what you are, and try to be that perfectly.'

Favourite verse: Matthew 28.20 'I am with you always, to the end of the age.'

Favourite woman: Martha, the sister of Mary and Lazarus. Why? She deserves redemption. She too often comes off worse in comparison with her sister Mary as she sits at Jesus' feet. She refreshingly challenges Jesus for not getting there sooner when Lazarus is ill and gives an immediate confession of faith, 'I believe that you are the Messiah, the Son of God, the one coming into the world' (John 11.27)) when Jesus responds. As Raymond E Brown's great commentary points out, this is the equivalent of Peter's 'my Lord and God'. Maybe Peter and Martha are not that dissimilar so why does Peter generally get a good press (he's impetuous but 'gets it' in the end) and Martha a bad press. Is she too strong a woman?

3

The Reverend Rose Hudson-Wilkin, Chaplain to the Speaker of the House of Commons

When Rose Hudson-Wilkin tells you she finds it as easy to talk to teenage gang members in East London as she does the Queen, it is easy to believe. I have rarely met anyone more comfortable in their own skin and with such natural warmth and presence. Being a Jamaican-born female priest must have led to some personal challenges, particularly in the male-dominated worlds of the Church and politics, but she rarely lets that show. There were some quite public difficulties around her appointment as the seventy-ninth Chaplain to the Speaker to the House of Commons but she is very popular with many of her colleagues even if her forthright views can annoy some people. Her pastoral skills are impressive and I was amused when a young man delivered an Easter egg during our meeting and was rewarded with a hug and a kiss. Looking at his face I imagine he likes an excuse to come by whenever he can.

Once I made it through security and the convoluted corridors of the Palace of Westminster, we sat down to talk in her cosy office, enhanced by Pugin's wooden panelling all around us. Rose leads a double life, one minute mingling with Britain's political leaders or saying a prayer at Lady Thatcher's funeral and then returning to a very different world as a vicar in Hackney in East London where she lives with her husband and grown-up children. She was recently made a prebendary at St Paul's Cathedral in recognition of her valuable work and service in the Diocese of London. She believes her upbringing in Jamaica is key to her confidence and it rapidly becomes clear when talking to her that her forthright views come from her wish to fight injustice of any kind and particularly to help those impacted by racism and misogyny.

'I was born and grew up in Montego Bay in Jamaica and I saw reflections of myself in all walks of life. We were sent to Sunday School and I was very much involved in the life of our little mission church of St Francis, which was part of the Anglican Communion family. We had Church Army officers who were in charge and the priests would parachute in for two Sundays per month. As young people we had the good fortune to be allowed to be involved in doing the readings, leading the intercessions and sometimes leading the Liturgy of the Word. I even got to preach as a teenager. Girls and boys were treated very fairly by our Sunday School teachers and I think they saw the potential gifts in all of us. I cut my teeth in this whole Minister thing there, in our local church, which is fantastic.

'My mother went to England shortly after I was born and I think the plan was that my father would join her and then we would join them because that's what families did at the time. But unfortunately when she came here she met someone else, got married and started a whole new family as she wasn't actually married to my father. So my oldest sister and I were left behind in Jamaica. But looking back now I thank God that we were because what I see from many Jamaican people of my age-group here, who were born here or who came over here and grew up here, was a real lack of confidence, a real disempowering of people who don't fully know exactly who they are. They don't see images of themselves in leadership or are not being allowed to be who they are because people look at you and think "That's the colour of your skin so that equates to x, y and z." Assumptions are made and people are kept in their corner.

'I think it was around the age of 14 when suddenly the going to church and Sunday school connected and made sense for me. I had this sense that my vocation was about being a minister of the Gospel although there weren't any there then. There were women who were Church Army sisters and I knew we had deaconesses but I also knew that they weren't fully in charge. I had the sense that I was going to be in charge and I was going to lead and I never doubted God. I remember thinking, "God, I believe you called me but I don't see women doing that so you're going to have to work it out." And he finally did in 1994 when women were first ordained.

'I say to folks that I didn't learn my theology at theological school. I did go to theological college but the foundation of my theology came from my folks, my aunt and the elderly people around me in the Church. What I saw there were people who had a real confidence in Christ, a genuine belief and trust. These were people who sometimes had nothing but they had everything. They were poor but they were joyful in the Lord. They knew that they were children of God and they brought us up to have that same trust and faith in God. When there was little money to buy things they would still say, "You don't worry about things like that. In God we trust, God will provide." And He would provide. If we had no food you could bet your boots somebody would turn up. We didn't have a telephone to phone anyone to say, "We have no food." But somebody who had a little bit of ground, we call it "gron" and had planted a bit of yam or callaloo and had a surplus of food, they would turn up. Or vice versa, we'd do the same. So this was about sharing and the sense of belonging in a community.

'I worked for a year after High School teaching RE and PE because my family couldn't afford to keep me and during that year I applied for the Church Army as an officer as I still had the sense of calling. At the time Church Army officers were only trained in England so I came over here in 1979 at the tender age of 18, knowing no one. It was a huge culture shock. I remember we were staying in Victoria for a few days before the college re-opened and I recall walking around and seeing people running and I'm thinking, "Where's the fire? I asked someone, "Is there a fire?" And they said, "No." I said, "Why are the people running?" "They're running to get their trains." And I thought, "How odd that they should be running to get their trains. In Jamaica the train waits for you."

'Also people were not warm, so not only was the climate cold but I thought people were cold. And I also thought people were not very caring. I remember being ill at a bus stop and I had to sort of bend on the floor. People stepped over me when the bus came and got on the bus, no one asked me if I was poorly. That would never happen in Jamaica. So those were strange times but I made some good friends and I even married one of them.

'I had come to college with a very simple faith that this is the Word of God. And I know when I was much younger I had a sense that God must have held somebody's hand and they never stopped writing from Genesis until Revelation. Of course, at theological college you learn that it didn't happen like this, that the Bible is a library, that it's written over hundreds of years. You learn that some of the things are allegorical or mythological. And that's tough, when all that has sustained you is suddenly ripped apart. And I would often go back to my room and cry and feel my world's falling apart. And then I remember pulling myself together and saying, "OK Rose, come on now. You are here to learn. What is the core of your faith?" And I thought, "OK, the core for me is that God created the world and actually I don't care whether he did it in seven days or 100 million." I believe nothing will ever shake that foundation that God created the world. When I see flowers and their designs, how intricate they are, that's no accident. I believe that God loves me and that he sent His son to die for me. I believe that I have life and that my life is not just about some heaven that is far away somewhere but that wherever I am with God that is heaven. So that then helps me to appreciate my theological learning experience. I was able to understand the fact that these things were written at a particular time and responding to a particular issue in the life of the Church. It doesn't make it irrelevant for me, but it makes me reflect on it to say, "OK, this was for them then, what might it be saying for me today?" There's some amazing stuff there but there's also some horrible stuff there too. I get very cross when those who are biblical fundamentalists say because it's there it has to be, it's just crazy.

'I finished my training at the college and went back to Jamaica. My husband Ken, who's a Geordie from the northeast of England, came out to visit me and we married there. We worked out there for a while but Ken decided he wanted to be ordained and that it wasn't fair for the Jamaican Church to pay for his training because he would one day want to come back to England. So he trained here on the Southwark Ordination

Course while he worked with John Sentamu (now Archbishop of York) who was a vicar in Tulse Hill.

'I applied for the Church during that time but the attitude of those when I applied, including my examining chaplain, an older woman, was that I should be looking after my husband and child. You think the Church would say we have very few ethnic minority clergy, so let's test her vocation, but instead it was "look after your husband and child", a rather crazy thing to do. I was two weeks away from delivering my second child when I was sent to see another examining chaplain. When I walked into his office I said to him, "I hope your midwifery skills are intact because I could deliver any moment." But he was fantastic; he never once asked me what I was going to do with my family. Interesting that the woman wanted to know but he wasn't interested in the least about that, we just talked theology.

'Meanwhile Ken was getting ready to move on and he got his first job in the Lichfield Diocese so we moved up there. I applied again through their system and things finally took off. I trained and was ordained as a deacon in 1991 and priest in 1994. I was in the first batch in the Diocese and it was a momentous occasion. But I describe it as giving birth, which is very painful. It was painful for me because when I came out of the Cathedral that day there were women there and I can still see one woman framed by the doorway, just leaning back and looking. And I could see in her eyes that here was someone who herself would have been ordained but was now too old. I felt that pain and it meant that my job was tempered. And I described it as giving birth and having this amazing child beside you but then you become aware that the woman in the next bed has lost her baby. That's what it felt like.

'I served my curacy in Wolverhampton but people initially didn't want me because they were from a particular Evangelical tradition. I believe they asked if they could have my husband instead of me. I went there knowing that and the Parish Church Council, I was told, had resigned on block. But I was determined that I would just go there and minister. I did something really foolish while I was there. Shortly after I got there I had to have knee surgery. When I came out of hospital I got my husband to drive me over to the parish and leave me and to come back and pick me up. I hobbled around on walking sticks and I remember distinctly thinking, "You know what, I'm going to do this because I don't want them to say 'she's a woman' or 'she's black, she can't hack it'." I was very aware that I was representing women and representing minority ethnic people. It's a huge burden but I had a real sense of responsibility.

'I stayed there for about four years before moving to West Bromwich, where I served part-time in the Parish of the Good Shepherd. And then the other part of my time I was Officer for Black Anglicans Concerns in the diocese. I was going around motivating minority ethnic people within the Church of England to say, "You need to be more than just sitting in the congregation. You've got gifts, don't just make the tea, don't just clean the church, be visible, don't rush home after church and do rice and peas. You have got to put yourself forward for PCC [Parish Church Council] and for Church Warden. You've got to put yourself forward for the Deanery and the Diocesan Synod." And I'd like to think that I still do that today. Recently an ordained woman of Asian origin said to me that one day she was at a crossroads in her life wondering what to do and I was on the television. She remembered thinking, "If she can do it, I can do that too." When women and young girls look at me I want them to say that.

'After that I came to Hackney in East London. My husband was looking for a post and I came along as a dutiful wife. He didn't think it was right for him but I thought it would be a great challenge. One of the churches was totally dilapidated inside and outside, overgrown with broken windows. It looked like a church that was no longer in use but it had about 12 to 15 people there worshipping. The other church had about half a dozen or so young black people being prepared for confirmation. That was part of the attraction too, that this is a multi-ethnic area and I wanted the young people in that area to have a model of themselves that was confident. It was important that they don't just see someone who is sweeping the streets when they come outdoors. So all that just screamed at me. Plus I like to get my hands dirty; I like to know that at the end of each day I've done a good day's work.

'A big challenge to me was that the church was very High Church and didn't want a woman. I had to go and see the representative of the Crown as it was a Crown appointment and he said to me, "Oh, you know, people are not sure. They would like you to come back for another interview." I refused. I'd picked up a hint that they didn't want me and I was sure that the black thing was an issue and I thought, "I'm not going to go and ingratiate myself before these people to beg and plead with them. They either have me or not." And he said yes so I was there. Two weeks later I met up with one of the wardens and I asked her to put all her cards on the table. "Has it got anything to do with the fact that I'm black?" And she said, "Well frankly, yes." So I said to them, "Well now that you've put your cards on the table, let me put mine on the table. I have just arrived here and I have no intention of rushing away, so you or anyone else who don't like me, either because I'm black or because I'm a woman, you're free to go. Furthermore, I'm very content and happy in my skin and in my gender." They didn't go immediately but they made life awkward because they would refuse to take Communion or they would come in and take part in part of the service and then walk out and ridiculous things like that. They eventually left and I thanked God. And the church has grown.

'It was a very challenging time but I never once doubted that I should be there. When the hand of God is on you then there's no need to doubt it. I'm very involved in the community with whatever is going on, supporting folks who've been involved with knife crime and families who've become victims of that as well. If I see a couple of lads blocking the sidewalk I don't go around them or cross the road, I go through them. And when I go through them I say, "Guys, I'm not meant to be asking you to move out of the way, come on now." I do engage with them. I get people knocking on my door at night-time and that can be challenging because my husband is very protective. He will say, "Darling you shouldn't be answering the door at that time of night." I say, "But darling, it's my vicarage and they expect to see the vicar if they knock." And I do open the door. In my reflection time I might think it isn't safe. I remember driving along one of the roads in the parish and I saw two young men fighting and one looked like he had a hammer in his hand. I jumped out of my car, engine running, and I'm right there in between them trying to get them apart. And after they separated I got back in the car and I was shaking at the thought of what I did but it never occurred to me in the process of doing it. All I could think of is somebody's either going to get done for murder or GBH [grievous bodily harm] or someone's going to be dead or be badly injured.

'When you work in a difficult place you have to love the people. People are not a nuisance. You must be there because you love the people and you feel a sense of calling to minister to them and to serve them. And so, whether I am standing in the pulpit preaching or whether I am cleaning up someone's toilet or cleaning up someone's diarrhoea or making a meal for someone, I love it. And I probably wouldn't know what to do with myself if I wasn't doing it. I work damn hard because I absolutely love what I do.'

Hearing Rose talk about her parish work with such enthusiasm made me wonder how she could cope with the formality of the Palace of Westminster. The role didn't seem to be an obvious fit for her skills and yet it has clearly been a success for her and for those who benefit from her chaplaincy. There was controversy in the press around the appointment and mixed views on the reasons behind that. She explained that it was when she had been in her parish for over a decade and there was refurbishment work to be done that she felt it was time to move on. Her husband told her about the post at Westminster Abbey and she explained her reaction.

'My knowledge of the Abbey was seeing people walking around in red robes which was not my idea of work but then I saw that it was a three-tiered job: Canon at the Abbey, Rector of St Margaret's Westminster and Chaplain to the Speaker. I thought that the chaplain part was just up my street because I believe passionately that faith should be in the public arena. Faith is not a garment to be put on when we feel like it or depending on the weather. This is who we are and I wanted to be there to encourage folks.

'I'm proficient at the liturgy so I had no anxiety with the performing part, because on those big stages that's what you do, in effect, in leading the liturgy. I am a Chaplain to Her Majesty the Queen and have spent a weekend at Windsor Castle so I am able to move between people of all different types. I was very comfortable in my skin doing that. So I did apply and I checked with the Dean that they would want a woman so I didn't waste my time. But of course there was all that furore because the Abbey felt that I wasn't what they wanted and Mr Speaker thought that I was ideal for the post. He said, "You walked into my room, you had presence, you were dynamic, I just had to have you." Bless him. I was disappointed that in the end they split the role. Previous Speakers and the Abbey in the past have not agreed on who should take on that role but they've always acquiesced to the Speaker, but on this occasion, no. I guess I wasn't male or white so that's why there was all that furore about it in the press. My colleague across the road became the Oxford graduate in one column and in the column adjoining I was the girl from Montego Bay.

'I decided to accept the job but it meant that I had no accommodation because the accommodation was in the Abbey cloisters. I had gone back to my parishioners and said to them, "Only part of the post has been given to me, would you be happy for me to stay on until I find something?" They were just delighted that they weren't losing me. I'm very happy but I'm under no illusion that this is extremely challenging because in effect I'm doing two full-time jobs. And I'm the type of person who doesn't know how to do things by half anyway. I think I'm already making a difference here. I do prayers every day in the Chapel and in the chambers when the House is sitting. And I meet and speak with Members, I'm available for those who want to come and see me pastorally. I do their weddings and their baptisms, not just for the Commons but also for the Lords. So it's like another parish but it's just got a specific kind of clientele different from my parish in Hackney.

'Politics is an aggressive, bruising and tough world. And I think there is still more to be changed. There are more women than there used to be but I am not necessarily convinced that it is 100 per cent women-friendly. I think it is still an old boys' domain and women will have to continue making huge sacrifices in order to continue being outstanding women constituency

MPs or in government. We have a saying in Jamaica that I'm telling you in English now, "If you want good, your nose will run." Your nose running is not a nice experience but you have to go through it.'

Rose liked to dip back into patois occasionally and even broke into song at one point as she enjoyed the chance to remember her formative years in Jamaica. In interviews she often refers to the issue of racism in the Church and the wider world in contrast to her own upbringing. I had read that she believes racism is a much bigger issue than homosexuality which takes up far too much of the Church's focus. She has asked the Church to apologise for its role in slavery and doesn't hold back on her language, even referring to the amendment in the women bishops' debate to allow men to ignore the authority of a female bishop as a kind of apartheid (*Telegraph* 5/2/2012).

'Racism exists because we are a fallen world. It is not just about people having a prejudice against black people, it is about people who, on top of the prejudice, have the power to decide whether you are good enough to be in this or that position. I want to see reflections of myself as I go through life but I am also aware that I live in a very diverse nation. It would feel very odd to me if I didn't see a broad reflection of society in the places where I go. I feel called to a place that reflects God's creation.

'I remember in Lichfield Diocese in my role as Officer for Black Anglican Concerns I asked a Church Warden, "If you had a vacancy here and I applied for it, would you consider me?" And she said, "Well, why would we consider you, we don't have any black people here?" I was fortunate to grow up in Jamaica where our motto is, "Out of many, one people." We have people from all different walks of life, Chinese, Indians, tourists coming and going, you name it they are there, but they are all Jamaicans. We grew up seeing a whole array of people and accepting people. Many come to a place like Britain which is supposed to be civilised only to find that people hold different thoughts. Racism does exist within the Church, but unfortunately we don't always name it for what it is. We say different things about it.'

Rose was also an outspoken advocate of women bishops in the debates. She stresses that she personally has no wish to be a bishop but is clear that the Church has lost out on the gifts of women as leaders. Her argument is more about justice than about advancing her own career and she thinks all this 'navel-gazing' is distracting the Church from the real crises in the world.

'I think we work together, male and female, as God created us. In Scripture Paul may have had a few rantings about women being silent in the Church but I believe that was in a particular context because the women were not allowed in the main part of the group and in Judaism the men were separate. Who knows for sure, we weren't there. But to then come and tell me now that I have to keep my mouth shut, that I'm not allowed to say anything of significance that a man might even possibly be able to learn from is absolutely ridiculous.

'As a Church, we have said that there are no theological reasons why women cannot be ordained. But what did we do? We agonised and fought and begrudgingly we let them become deacons. Let more years go by of agonising and then we begrudgingly say, "OK, we'll let them become priests." And then we are fighting again, and arguing and begrudgingly, "OK, maybe they can become bishops if you give me all these packages to make sure I am not tainted by them." What the hell am I going to do to a grown man or a grown woman, why they need to be protected from me? Stop all this silliness. And I have very little patience, I'm afraid, with the Church leadership that tries to pat these people on the head and say, "Oh, we understand you." Please, stop that nonsense.

'I felt numb when the vote was lost (in 2012) but I didn't really believe it was going to go through. I've always said it won't happen in my lifetime. Throughout all that week the verse and scripture that kept sustaining me was Habakkuk 3.17–19: "Though the fig tree does not blossom, and no fruit is on the vines; though the produce of the olive fails, and the fields yield no food … yet I will rejoice in the Lord." This silliness isn't going to prevent me from knowing who called me and what I'm called to do. They cannot take that away from me. I also have this wonderful thing that my tears are special and I won't allow you to see them, especially if you are the one that is pressing. I remember an elderly lady saying to me that she had voted against having a woman priest in her church because Sundays was the only day that she got to see and touch a man. And I remember saying to her, "I'm so proud of you, I can respect you for voting in the way you did. You're the first person to give me a really rational reason for voting against women." I can respect that but those who are going around clothing their stupidity and their silliness in theological garments, it's crazy.'

My experience as a trustee of the Christian international relief and development charity Tearfund has taught me that women in developing countries often suffer disproportionately to men, whether from poorer health and a lack of education or as a result of violence and domestic abuse. Knowing the influence of the Church in countries like Africa I wondered if Rose felt the Church had failed to take the lead on solving some of these issues and how she speaks out when she sees injustice around her.

'I think to some extent the Church has contributed to the poor treatment of women around the world. Because if you teach that women are not as important as men and as if God is saying that, to a community that is sometimes illiterate, then you are doing a huge disservice. If women are not being educated to teach their boys that women are just as important as they are, then we have a crisis. We see a situation where men think that by the very nature of having their genitals different from us, it means that they can be abusive.

'There was a time when the Church didn't take violence against women seriously. I went to the World Council of Churches Meeting in Zimbabwe and we had a women's conference beforehand. I was appalled when I heard women saying that they would go to their priest to complain about their husbands beating them and the priest just wanted them to accept it and then there are priests who beat their wives. The Church has no integrity, speaking to others about discrimination and justice if it does not exercise that itself. By maintaining an all-male domain here, the signal that you're sending out is that women are second-class.

'We need to start valuing people and to teach young boys and girls to respect each other as their equals. Of course we're different, I'm not trying to be a man. I am just so pleased that

I'm a woman but I'm my husband's equal. My husband has never in our 30 years together said that he is the head of the household. How ridiculous he would sound. We are two adults within the home, we have children and we are both responsible. If he feels strongly about something then we go with it, if I feel strongly then we go with it. Sometimes we both feel strongly and we have a little impasse or two but something works itself out.

'I do feel passionately about lots of things and I don't believe I should be silent. I think that one's got a gift to speak and it's not a gift that you take and lock away in the bottom drawer. And I think that when you've got a gift of leadership much is required of you. I speak on behalf of people and I don't like to see injustices. I will accompany people to speak to authority as I do not like to see the poor downtrodden by those who think that they are in authority and see you're just a nuisance. I think I have been given that gift to be able to speak so I must use it.

'The reality is this is not an ordinary job, it's a vocation. I am there 24/7 and that carries its own costs. I'm always ready. I guess my Church Army evangelistic training stood me in good stead. You have to have that call deep inside your gut to be able to walk in that direction and to follow in the footsteps of Christ, to be able to pray daily and to be able to love even the prickly people that come in your direction. Because all those wretched folks who say no to you because you're a woman, you've still got to love them. It is not an option. I say to young women, "Listen to that still small voice. And if you hear it do not be afraid to say 'yes'. The world may tell you 'no', because you're a woman but don't forget you're not answering to them, you're answerable to God." And so I have no regrets that I gave my life to the Church.'

As our time together drew to a close I sensed her anger with the Church but also her determination not to blame people who she feels are ignorant in their prejudice. I feel sad for her that she wasn't given the full role at Westminster which would have allowed her to live with her family close to the heart of the political world. Somehow her outspokenness and political awareness seem ideally suited to this environment. Both the Church and government are heavily represented in Parliament

Square but it seems ironic that she is only really welcome in the political space. To me, Rose is a tremendous force for good in the wider world. She doesn't hesitate to hold a mirror up to the prejudices and judgements that so easily become part of our everyday lives and to live out the Gospel in the place where she has been called. We can be glad that the girl from Jamaica found her calling in England.

Favourite verse: 1 John 4.20 *'Those who say, "I love God", and hate their brothers or sisters, are liars; for those who do not love a brother or sister whom they have seen, cannot love God whom they have not seen.'*

Favourite woman: Ruth. In Ruth 1.16 she says 'Do not press me to leave you ... Where you go, I will go; where you lodge, I will lodge; your people shall be my people, and your God my God.' She for me is the embodiment of how I do ministry. I journey alongside my parishioners. They become my fathers and mothers, my sisters and brothers as well as my children.

4

The Reverend Vivienne Faull, Dean of York

Vivienne Faull is one of the most senior women in the Church of England and was the first woman to lead a cathedral. Now in her late 50s, she exudes the confidence, focus and authority of the finest CEO, but like so many of the women I meet in the Church that is not the whole story. We first met in her modern, functional office in a building behind the magnificent York Minster but it was when we walked across to the impressive Minster itself that I saw the other side of Vivienne. She loves the building for its light and its femininity, the sense that its elaborate decoration makes it look as though it 'has its best clothes on'.

In a way Vivienne too came to life in the building and as she showed me the place where she had been 'unveiled' to the congregation with all the symbolism of that moment, I was struck by her femininity and charm but also by a sense of her fragility. She showed me the lovely Zouche Chapel now set aside for private prayer and explained that when she first arrived for morning prayers it was winter and always dark, so she couldn't make out the detail of the stained-glass windows opposite her chair. She felt it was rather symbolic that the morning the new Pope was announced the sun flooded through the windows and she realised she was looking at St Francis – the name taken by the new Pope Francis.

Vivienne has had an impressive career in the Church and took a lead role in the legislation for women bishops so she must have found the failure of the vote in November 2012 a huge setback. I had read that she saw her relationship with the Church as both affectionate and subversive, and she had certainly had her share of unpleasant hate mail. She is married to Michael, a hospital consultant, and has the challenge of living between two places, York and Leicester, where he still lives and works. She began by telling me about her background and her calling.

'I grew up on the Wirral and went to a school in Chester. I had connections through school with the life of faith but much more particularly through my parents. My father was a vet and had been raised as a Methodist, and mother was raised as an Anglican. Both of them have remained part of the Church throughout their lives and my father was eventually ordained as a Methodist Minister. We had been part of the life of local churches for as long as I could remember and I was very fortunate in having that sort of background. When I got into the sixth form the rather formidable headmistress said she could get me into Oxford to read theology, but because I am a determined sort of person I decided I was going to do history, which was what I loved and saw as a proper subject. She could see that I was interested in the life of faith and could handle it academically.

'Once I was at Oxford I started going to church at St Aldates, which was immensely lively as it is now, at the liberal end of evangelicalism and beginning to be affected by the charismatic movement. It was a very encouraging place. It didn't have a radical stance on the place of women in ministry but there were significant female role models there including two full-time women lay workers doing pastoral and teaching work who were ordained later. One was June Osborne who is now Dean of Salisbury. Ordination was being discussed at the time but there were other priorities for the Church.

'During my final year at St Aldates we used to go on missions which I wasn't at all sure about but the leader of our youth team suggested I might do this full-time. He gave me a card for the Church Pastoral Aid Society and said, "They help people to think through what their vocation might be and I think you ought to be a deaconess rather than a parish worker because the pension is better". That was the first time anybody had said directly that there is a possibility here that you ought to consider. I probably had thought of it myself but at that stage there weren't obvious routes into the Church for a woman and I was considering becoming a lawyer or possibly a teacher.

'In terms of a calling I think my family always assumed that whatever we did you needed to have a sense of vocation, whether it was to church work or not. I think my father had felt he had a vocation to be the best possible vet that he could be and my mother to be the best possible college lecturer that she could be, so we didn't make that split between sacred and secular. It was all going to be about vocation and there just wasn't a framework in the 1970s for women to think of a vocation except for the deaconess communities which were only just starting to come out of their almost monastic existence into parishes.

'Whilst I was thinking about working my way through the Church of England selection processes I decided to see what I might do outside Great Britain that was completely different. So the week before I went to my Church of England selection conference I went to a Church Mission Society selection conference and they decided to send me off to India for a couple of years. The Church agreed, although I think they wanted to send me straight off to theological college. This was 1977 and there was just a sense around that there was a movement to encourage women more overtly into ministry. Sex discrimination legislation was beginning to come into effect and there was a general cultural change that was starting to encourage women to do things that previously had been impossible. It was also about encouraging men to encourage women as well which meant women had advocates in that rather soft liberal feminism of the middle and late 1970s.

'So I went off to India with a friend in 1977 for what turned out to be 18 months. We came back slightly early because things in Afghanistan were starting to get difficult and there was a bit of concern that we might be a bit too isolated and vulnerable where we were in the north of India. And then I went to live and work in a place called Shrewsbury House in Liverpool, where there were other folk who I had known from university and we lived in community together. It was a time of intense economic difficulty for this country and half of Liverpool was unemployed and to experience living in Everton during that acute economic deprivation was a very important experience for me. I had lived in one of the poorest places in India and then came back to one of the poorest places in England.

'Both those experiences were cross-cultural. I learnt to live in very different sorts of environments and found that though they were demanding I could thrive. I think those two experiences have given me the confidence to think that wherever I am I can find ways of "being" that allow me to flourish, sometimes more, sometimes less. But that has made the process of moving into otherwise apparently uncomfortable situations easier than they might otherwise have been. I think the experience in India with the two of us feeling quite isolated because there was no official church was also useful. I was a class teacher working with 40 girls and boys in a township that was attached to a local oil refinery, which was an attempt by the Indian government to industrialise the state of Bihar. Trickle-down economics doesn't particularly work but it did bring a lot of skilled workers into that area and the school was there to resource those communities. The teachers by and large came from Christian backgrounds but there was no church. We worshipped in the school hall and a Church of North India priest came once a month, so I had to learn how to find the spiritual resources to keep going. Things like saying morning and evening prayer and the sense that there was a community of faith beyond that immediate community was very important. It wasn't just cultural but also spiritual resilience that I discovered at that point.

'Having come back to England and been accepted for training I was trying to find my way into a theological college and was encouraged to go to St John's Nottingham, but the problem was that the Church of England didn't recognise St John's Nottingham to train women. Women were at that stage only allowed to train in a very small number of theological authorities, the theory being that you had to have a peer group around.

'I had grown up in the 1960s and 1970s and I realised that unless women trained alongside the men at all the theological colleges there was no way that we were ever going to be accepted. And there were three or four of us who were just pushing the doors of the theological colleges and seeing which ones would open and I was very fortunate. I went to look around St John's Nottingham and the acting Principal admitted that he wasn't sure where he stood on the ordination of women but he thought that it would be a jolly good idea if I went there because he was always the entrepreneur. It took several months to fix and I had a very happy three years there with very inspirational teachers. We had students from Uganda and we had students from South Africa, black, white and coloured, who had been sent out by the Church in South Africa to prepare for the day when apartheid ended. It felt as if we were on the verge of all sorts of changes and that included the place of women in the Church's ministry. I was elected student vice-president and then student president so I actually led the community through that time and it felt very happy.

'I was sponsored by the Diocese of Chester and I thought I had been selected to train as a deaconess but the Church of England thought I had been selected to train as a parish worker. The main difference was that deaconesses were in some sort of holy order whereas parish workers were very definitely lay workers. And so when I was coming towards the end of my time at St John's I had to start looking for a job but there really wasn't a system for the women. I remember the person in charge of women and their ministry in Chester Diocese sent me a list of all the incumbents in the diocese and said, "Here is a list of incumbents, by all means write to them and ask if they would like a deaconess, but this doesn't guarantee you any money." So I realised this wasn't going to be straightforward but after looking at some jobs in different places I ended up at a parish in Liverpool and it was the right decision, the right place at the right time.

'Liverpool had encouraged women in ministry for a long time to the extent that they had women on the staff of the cathedral so women weren't an innovation there as they would have been in some places. And so I went as an extra pair of hands in the parish in Mossley Hill where most of the university students or halls of residence were. The university chaplain was attached to the church so we had quite a big team and it was a really good place to learn.

'Towards the end of my three years as a deaconess there I wondered what to do next. Again we weren't very deployable. Editing the diocesan newsletter and being chaplain to the women's hospital and a part-time attachment to a parish was one option but I was with one of my fellow curates and he said, "I have just seen this job advertised at Clare College, Cambridge. They clearly want a black lesbian nun and you are at least a bit closer to them. Have a look at the details." And so I did and put in an application, thinking I would get nowhere. I was interviewed and had the most extraordinary experience because the interview took about half an hour or so with a panel and then half an hour with the Director of Music and then that was it. I didn't meet a student as it was out of term. And when I walked into the house the Master was on the phone offering me the job. By that stage the thought of leaving Liverpool was quite tough because it was a city going through very difficult times and my parish was being made redundant almost at that time. I was doing a job where I felt as though I was doing something useful and all of a sudden to be offered a job in what felt a very privileged place was something I struggled with ethically. But then the Dean at the time was Rowan Williams and he phoned me up and said, "I am sorry we clearly didn't handle this very well, you didn't get a chance to get to know us, do you want to come back and have a look?" And after another week or so thinking about it I decided to take the job.

'I wasn't ordained but the college thought that was a huge advantage in the sense that they could show off. Clare College is a lovely liberal community and to have a woman chaplain was great. They used to tease visitors because obviously I wasn't wearing a dog collar so they could disguise the fact I was a chaplain and all these people would arrive assuming that they were looking for a male figure.

'In 1987 I was ordained as a deacon in the Diocese of Ely, which meant I could do weddings and at long last became a bit more useful around the college. It was a big change culturally because we started wearing dog collars and that was the thing that shifted the public perception. I am aware that colleges and cathedrals are immensely seductive places and I was at a college that had a very strong community life but after five years I felt it was time to move on. My next role was as chaplain at Gloucester Cathedral. I had four years there, got married to Michael and I was ordained as a priest there. It's very interesting because people in Gloucester remember me very fondly and I think it is partly that they felt as if they had enabled me to get married and to be ordained and that sense of co-ownership was lovely. Gloucester was going through a difficult time then. There was real deprivation and a real issue about faith and race in the city because there was a longstanding black community which wasn't well integrated and increasing numbers of Asians arriving.

'When it came to our ordination as priests we had quite a bumpy time as women in the diocese because a new bishop, Peter, came after I arrived and said he wasn't going to ordain women, which led to a lot of upset. He would have ordained us in the end but things happened to him and so he was removed. And then the diocese got very cautious and I remember our Diocesan Bishop saying we would have to go through the selection process. All he wanted was for us to have a conversation with someone about our journey of faith but he put it in terms of a selection conference. There were women who were ordained with me in Gloucester who had been in ministry since the 1950s and for a new bishop to say we are sending you back to selection when all of us had been through several selection conferences already made us absolutely furious.

'And the Bishop then chose the feast of St Matthias for the day of our ordination and Matthias was the apostolic substitute chosen after Judas had killed himself. It just didn't go well really, nevertheless the actual occasion was great and there were two ordination services. Bishop Peter sent us a lovely message saying, "I am sorry I am not with you, I would have ordained you with joy." That for many of us felt more significant than anything else. I presided at the Eucharist for the first time at the main Sunday morning service so it was quite an ordeal really. Gloucester Cathedral was immensely supportive but the pressures were very significant. You know if you do something badly it is because you are a woman but if you do it well it is just because of you as an individual. I think that has changed a bit in the last few years but certainly at that stage we were clearly being observed in all sorts of ways.

'After this I went to Coventry for six years as a residential Canon Pastor and then as Vice Provost and I had to run the cathedral for a year when the provost was on sick leave. There was a lovely moment when I presided at the Eucharist for the first time in Coventry and I went, "The Lord is here" and the spotlights blew with this huge bang and I was not sure whether I had been shot but I was still standing there so we just carried on and it was a source of great hilarity.

'And then I went to Leicester in 2000 as Provost and became the first woman to take charge of a cathedral as a Dean in 2002. Leicester Cathedral was in a really difficult place so it was hard. My senior Canon was opposed to the ordination of women and so it was really tricky on all fronts for the first five years, which was why I stayed quite a long time because I wanted to get into the good times as well. By about 2005 it all started to get better and it became a very exciting place to be but it took a long time to do the basic groundwork. I discovered there was real misogyny around, although not actually in the Church. I was blackballed for a job in another cathedral by somebody in wider civil society. At that stage the Crown made those appointments, having made enquiries but not telling the candidate that they were under consideration and they phoned somebody and that person said negative things. It took several years for me to realise that it wasn't personal but it was gender-based because that person did it to other people as well in different ways. And of course the men didn't experience it, so even my closest senior colleagues and bishop staff assumed it was because I had done something wrong. Of course there are misjudgements you make in the early stages of learning your job but, as I say, it was only towards the end of my time that I could name what had gone on as a real abuse of power.

'I remain very fond of the senior Canon but he wouldn't vest as a priest if I was presiding, he would wear choir dress and would bring his own chalice and paten. It didn't feel personal because I had known him for a long time and in fact he previously had been very supportive of women priests but changed his mind on the day of the vote in 1992. And his colleague, the Residentiary Canon, had been opposed until that vote in 1992 and then he decided because it was the will of the Church he would be in favour. So these two Canons who sat next door to each other swapped places on that issue on that day which was very curious. But what became very difficult was holding the staff team together because they were very angry with the way that the senior Canon behaved and thought that it was completely unwarranted, so I had to spend a lot of my time containing that anger. And that is why it took a long time to get the place sorted out because you can't do a lot of strategic work when you have got a team that is at war with itself about the nature of the leadership they are under. It was also important for the Bishop and I to keep things together in a very complex environment and we had to work really hard at it.

'I was also quite isolated, not least because I think it was another couple of years before June Osborne was appointed as another Dean and the role itself means you are both chairman and chief executive. You hold all the responsibility for both the spiritual and administrative life and you have to work to make sure they are not divorced. Increasingly we are seeing that cathedrals are powerful because people come on some sort of spiritual quest. So it is a question of trying to run the place to respond to what God is doing here and with that as the primary purpose and to make sure that the business model can enable that to happen. While I was at Gloucester I started doing an MBA which took me quite a long time to finish because of other priorities, but I learnt how to do the business stuff at the service of the Church. In York I am running a major business but it is a business with a purpose.

'York Minster would be typical of most cathedrals. We start the day with prayer at 7.30 a.m. and finish with choral evensong at 5.15 p.m. and then we go home to emails. But the day is framed and begins and ends with prayer so you don't forget that is what you are about. At different stages different things stress you. I was very interested in observing myself when I was unveiled here and for a lot of people the size of the building would be quite stressful but I actually quite enjoy it. What stresses me is having to do too much in too short a time and not doing it well enough.

'I am formally a member of the Archbishop of York's staff. My job as Dean is to keep this place secure for him to exercise his ministry. I will not do anything to threaten or disrupt him and if I do that it is inadvertent. And that means that some of the things that I might have been able to campaign on previously I won't now. I think it has taken me a time to find my voice here, particularly in preaching, to know where I can push the boundaries as there is something about being a role model. The number of men and women who have come to me who have said, "This is such a significant appointment for us. You are carrying such a lot for us." If you play those sorts of hierarchical games then I am meant to be the most senior woman in the Church of England but I don't feel that pressure because it just sounds blasé or impertinent. I am used to having to carry the pioneering label and it feels much less stressful now than it did in Leicester and possibly than it did even in Cambridge.

'The role of the Cathedral, according to research, is very significant because they seem to carry meaning for individuals and that is way beyond people who call themselves Anglicans or Christians as they become places of pilgrimage for people of all sorts of different faith communities. And it is quite clear that although the media think that we live in a secular country, if you look at the behaviour of what is going on here that is not the case. Not just that, cathedrals are places that invest meaning in the locality. We normally charge for entrance but on Good Friday we have a free day and 6,300 people came through the doors this year. Easter Sunday morning nearly 2,000 people came to worship, Christmas morning 3,000 people came to worship. We are not making any concessions culturally or in any other way, it is just that people are looking for something.'

Although Vivienne has had a stellar career in the Church of England and has managed to remain calm and stoical in many challenging situations, I was sure that the failure of the debate on women bishops in 2012 must have hurt her personally. She played a very significant role in the debate, earning the respect of many of her male and female colleagues over many years and has a personal insight that few others would have. She clearly felt the outcome would have significant repercussions for women across the world but is hopeful for a solution as the culture has shifted.

'I led the legislation for the debate and I had spent the last 12 years trying to put together a legislative package that would get enough votes and it failed so I was very involved and it felt personal. We started at a very basic level looking at the theology. I was part of the Rochester Commission, working through what sort of package we wanted to put together, not just in terms of women being bishops but with provision made for those who couldn't accept that. It became more and more difficult not least because, to be honest, neither Archbishop was really on side at that point nor was the House of Bishops, bless them. Personally they are absolutely on side but institutionally it was clear that those who were opposed particularly from an Anglo-Catholic perspective had the ear of the archbishops. For Rowan I think it was the fear of being treated as a sect rather than a church. He has strong links with the Orthodox Church and the sense that he would no longer have that sense of brotherhood with them, I think he found really difficult to handle. That said, he had appointed me and he had always been immensely supportive and always said, "I want women to be bishops." It just felt that in his heart that wasn't where he was. Since the vote we are in a very different place. What that means in terms of legislation is a different question but it feels culturally different, not least because of the national backlash.

'The Church does look like a shambles. If they can't make a decision about this then they can't make a decision about any difficult issue, because this is not the most difficult issue we face and I don't mean gay clergy. I actually think the most difficult thing is the pastoral reorganisation of what we do with the huge number of churches that are costing a huge amount of money for us to run. It is a bit like trying to close a hospital in an area, each time they make a decision in principle the local area rises up and says, "no you can't do that". Now working all that through is going to be much, much more difficult than these kind of ethical issues and if we can't deal with the big ethical issues we are going to be nowhere really.

'On the day of the vote I didn't think it would go wrong. We knew we had the House of Clergy and the House of Bishops but we hadn't done all our homework on the House of Laity. When the vote was announced we all knew that it was very serious politically. I was due to go live on Channel 4 and that was the point at which I realised I had thought it was going to go through and I realised I couldn't go straight onto Channel 4 News because I didn't have anything to say.

'There were others on the steering group who were in tears, but there was a lovely moment later in the evening at a farewell dinner for the legislative committee where we inaugurated the "dead measure" society. At one point there was a kind of necessary "girly" moment when two of us ended up in tears in the loo and I think both of us needed that time apart, until we were interrupted by a High Court judge saying, "Now come on you two." That was just what we needed but it was pretty dreadful. I had just moved house to York, dumped my things, gone to London. I came back and had to go straight into preparing for my installation here. It was weird really trying to handle a Church of England that felt as if it was in a very different place. It was my last day on General Synod as well. When it finally happens, the Church will just look like the rest of British society instead of looking like something that is left over from the nineteenth century.

'There is this huge debate about what is to do with gender and what is to do with the personality in terms of the change in the culture of an institution. My sense is that the Church has always changed and continues to change. The House of Bishops is currently changing, they have passed this resolution that eight senior women shall be members of the House of Bishops, non-voting members, and the paper talked about those women bringing the culture change but I think it is already happening. There was a very moving statement in the current working group by a friend of mine who is the Bishop of Rochester now, who said, "Where I want to start from is the fact that Viv and I started at Oxford on the same day, and I think it is completely unacceptable that I can wear a purple shirt and she can't." And I have never heard a bishop put it quite as forcefully as that and I found that immensely moving. It is a generation who have grown up as men who don't want to be in this peculiar situation of an all-male club any longer.

'I also don't think at the moment the Church can say anything with a degree of integrity at all about the abuse of women across the world. Canon Jane Charman gave an interesting speech in which she said: "This is not actually in the end a debate about Vivienne Faull and June Osborne or Rose Hudson-Wilkin and whether they should be bishops, this is about all those women across the world who today will die as a result of abuse. This is about who women are and their relationship with God and their relationship with their fellow human beings." And I think it is right to pitch it at that level. This is theological anthropology, are women really people? That is the debate. I think wider society in the nearly 20 years since I was ordained as a priest has got ahead of the Church and has decided that women really are people. Ghastly things happen in this country but they are recognised as ghastly and they are recognised as something that needs to be changed. In the rest of the world there are areas where women are not yet regarded as fully human beings and that is what the Church should be proclaiming. The Church should be an instrument of subversion and of transformation, and at the moment it can't do that because it is failing to offer women a full place in the life of the leadership of the Church.

'In parishes I think women have brought differences in terms of pastoral accessibility and the ease of relating to all sorts of people. That is not to say men haven't got that, quite a lot have it and some will do it much better than women, but it is a different sort of model. Above all I think that in having women as priests people have begun to see that God is rather bigger than God was perceived, God is not just perceived of in male form now. So I think the stuff about iconography is very significant and I see the change here. When I arrived at York Minster I was the first woman to preside at the main altar and I found that absolutely shocking. Nearly 20 years on from the ordination of priests no woman had presided here, they were still in la-la land. It was clear when I presided for the first time there was quite a lot of anxiety around the place and holding that space on that day was really quite difficult.'

I sensed an underlying anger at the difficulties women have had to face over the years. Vivienne had suffered her share of abuse as one of the most visible women in the Church. She had admitted to suffering from anorexia at Oxford and I wondered how she coped with the kind of stress that can come with her role now and whether she was always as confident as she might have looked to others.

'I remember my mother saying [when I was at Oxford], "You have lost such a lot of weight." And it was clearly the stress ...

well it was a bit more than that, it had become a bit habitual. And I had to learn how to live on my own because it was when I was single and just not eating and then realising that not eating perhaps gave me a bit more control than eating. So I had to be quite careful not to go back to that.

'I think one of the things you learn is how to busk. I remember going into the job in Leicester and saying to the bishop, "I am just not prepared for any of this." And he said, "None of us are." All of us men and women who are perfectionists and want to have everything sorted find it humbling when you suddenly realise you are in a job where you can't sort it all and perhaps it is just not the right sort of framework to be thinking like that anyway. Because then you have to say it is up to God what God can do with this mess and it is something to do with grace at that point.

'I have had a lot of abusive personal stuff, abusive and pornographic letters in the past, so in a sense I am relatively resilient to that kind of thing now. I always assumed this is my battle but actually it is not – it is society's battle. But I am worried that it is happening because of what it signifies about what is going on in wider society. And particularly with social media, now things can blow up so fast and so my friend [Professor] Mary Beard's terrible experience of horrific online abuse after *Question Time* in Leicester [January 2013] is symptomatic of what can happen to any woman in a leadership position who happens to step out of line in the sense of saying something courageous.

'There is also something about the experience of being on the margins that I think has brought quite a lot to leadership for women in my generation. Some have been immensely hurt by that marginalisation, others like me have discovered that actually it is quite an interesting place to be on the margins, it is sometimes the place where all sorts of things are happening that are exciting and new. Women have been marginalised in the life of the Church, gay people have been marginalised, black people have been marginalised and I think they bring something extraordinary in that experience.'

I found Vivienne's honesty about the difficulties of being a woman in a leadership position very moving. I am certain there would be women in all kinds of professions who would relate to her way of thinking and recognise the effort required to be a pioneer and role model for so many other women who have followed her into the Church. Yet again I am struck by the courage of women like Vivienne but I am also reminded that unlike many other professions this is about having a genuine calling and a deep faith. Personally I thank God that she cares so much about the future role of women everywhere that she was found weeping in the ladies' loo after the debate ended so disastrously.

Favourite verse: Ruth 1.16 'Where you go I will go, and where you stay I will stay' (NIV).

Favourite woman: Ruth. In the first chapter of the book of Ruth she says to Naomi 'Where you go I will go.' She makes this vow as a foreign woman travelling with Naomi and it is so significant because she doesn't know what it is going to cost. It is about the way God transcends all the boundaries that we set up about gender and race and faith and does something new.

5

The Reverend Tamsin Merchant

Tamsin Merchant is Vicar of St Mary's Hornsey Rise in North London and is the youngest woman in this book. I was interested in whether her perception of the role of women in the Church would be any different as she is from a newer generation who often feel less constrained by the rules of the Church. At the same time her background as an evangelical could have made it much less likely for her to be ordained. She is seen by fellow evangelicals as one of the leaders of the future and, as we spoke, she was involved in organising a conference called 'Young Women and the Church'. The event is aimed at encouraging young women, particularly from an evangelical background, who feel they may have a calling to be ordained. Although almost 50 per cent of ordinands today are women they tend to be from a much older generation, whereas in the younger age group the numbers are more disappointing.

Tamsin lives with her husband and two dogs in a comfortable vicarage next to her church, decorated with some of her own impressive artwork. She is very charming and a natural leader but with a good dose of humility mixed in. Her faith really shines out and it is easy to imagine she will go far in the Church but the challenge will be balancing the many calls on her time. Her husband teaches at St Mellitus College alongside Jane Williams (Chapter 7) and, although a vicar himself, he has been very supportive of her calling. Tamsin had a solid background in the Church, as she explained to me when we met.

'I was born in Birmingham. My dad is a vicar and from a very early age I would say that I experienced a sense of the presence of God and that God was with me, which gave me confidence. The Church I was part of in my teens had a really good youth group so you could cope with the fact that not everything in a

73

Sunday service was interesting. Instead you had your own things that were more interesting such as boys and sport and there was Bible study and plenty of singing. Probably a key turning point for me was going on Scripture Union camps, which meant I was able to get away from home and family and was more able to ask questions.

'My dad worked at St Helen's Bishopsgate in London as his second curacy and he was very involved in seeing a lot of people from public schools come to faith and he helped set up an organisation called the Stewards Trust [which runs informal house parties to promote and encourage the Christian faith]. I went on holiday weeks with them from about the age of seven, even though I went to a grammar school. I had this sort of funny bizarre world where I could go to my school in Birmingham and I'd talk Brummie and then I'd go on to these Stewards Trust house parties where I think they just thought I was quite odd but they could love me anyway. I didn't fit the mould because all the girls had this beautiful long hair and by that stage I was there with my spiked punk look that all my friends had at school. Those experiences were really good because they taught me social skills, as well as providing me with a place to explore my faith. They taught me how to speak to anyone because you learnt that it was about being warm and welcoming rather than how you looked.

'Then when I was about 15 or so I started to go to a youth group that was much more local and ecumenical. There were up to about 50 of us in the end and it was unusual in that the young people took an active leadership role, so we led all the small group discussions and the worship. There was a couple who oversaw it and they probably pulled their hair out fairly regularly. At the same time that that happened I finally went along to the school Christian Union, having avoided it for almost my entire school time, thinking it was really boring. About 20 of us met every day for prayer before school and I used to go along too. I still look back and can't believe that I used to get up and be at school for 8.15 to pray and do Bible study. It used to make me laugh because we'd be the ones getting into trouble being late for registration because we'd been praying. I think those two things were really key for me in terms of beginning to

exercise leadership and to have the guts to step out and do some
things that were outside my comfort zone.

'The school I went to was very much about going on to
university, but I liked art and music and didn't really fit in. I
didn't want to go to university for the sake of it so I decided
to work for Jackie Pullinger in Hong Kong [founder of the St
Stephen's Society providing rehabilitation for drug addicts]. My
father knew her and I had read her book *Chasing the Dragon*
when I was about nine and thought she was amazing. My
brother had been there for three months, so after school I went
out there for a year to work in one of the first-stage houses in a
little village on Lantau Island and it really blew my brains out.

'I think at the age of 18, having grown up in Birmingham in a
nice family in a pretty nice environment, walking into the stage
house was a shock. It was where the men that they'd met would
come to get off heroin, so my first experience really was going
and living amongst these men aged from 19 to 60 and some had
been on heroin for five or six years or even up to 30 years. Jackie
had a church called St Stephen's and they used to do meetings
in this one area where a lot of the drug addicts hung out and so
they'd come to the meetings and that would be their way into
rehab, and they worked on the principle that you just pray for
them and they have ten days to come off heroin. Well it does
take ten days for the body to get rid of heroin so they'd always
have someone with them for 24 hours a day who'd pray with
them and help them through it.

'And this was the extraordinary bit for me, both that I was
only 18 and that someone let me go out and do this. I was
asked if I spoke Cantonese and I said, "No, it's not really on
the curriculum at my school," and they said, "Good, because
now you have to show them Jesus." And I thought, "Oh no,
what do you mean I've got to show them Jesus? Like how?"
And of course it was actually just about being loving and kind
and gentle and offering friendship, and when you were with
someone coming off heroin you would be with them the whole
time and you were encouraged to pray with them all the time
either quietly or in tongues.

It was terrifying. I still remember walking up there and all
these guys were sitting on the railings and I was thinking, "Can

I go home now?" But because of all the experiences I had as a teenager, all these different environments, I thought, "No, what you do is you walk up and you smile and you say, 'Hi, I'm Tamsin'," and I did that and then of course discovered that although they'd all been on heroin and a lot of them had been in prison, they were still just people. I was told, "Here you are, you're looking after Ah Sing and he's come off heroin and you've got to pray with him," and I'm thinking "OK, it'll be on my watch that he has a nightmare and it's a disaster and he'll be full of pain." But the amazing thing was that God seems to work through prayer to help people come off heroin out there, and it happens again and again and again. I guess if you're looking at it scientifically you could wonder if it has become a self-fulfilling psychosomatic thing. But what I did know was that the men coming off knew what it was like to come off 'cold turkey' and they would still sit there and that was often the point when some of them would actually come to faith because they'd signed up to this programme because they wanted help. But the moment they discovered that God would help even them through prayer was the time when some of them went, "OK, maybe I need to take notice of this Jesus person." And Jackie's big thing was, "They don't need to know all the stuff about Church, they just need to know Jesus, keep it simple." And so that helped because I didn't feel like I had to know huge amounts of theology, I just had to know the person of Jesus and the stories about Jesus, and I knew those so that was amazing.

'Overall it was pretty successful because the men would go from there into the second stage where they'd begin to learn how to live in a normal world and some would get work or continue to help. I got to go back there about six years ago with my work for a conference and what I loved was seeing someone who had stayed true to their calling of helping the poor and the people at the bottom of the pile. Jackie is quite amazing – she could have built a cool church full of really rich people but it was still full of people who were at the bottom, as well as people with amazing degrees. It's a mix, but actually the heart of what she did was still about, "It's these people who need Him most."

'After that experience in Hong Kong I came back to do a Fine Art degree at Byam Shaw School of Art in London [now part of Central St Martin's College] and that was when I really discovered I had a brain. I was made to think, I was made to ask questions and it challenged me creatively, and it also challenged my faith because it was a small college. There weren't many other Christians but there were lots of people with questions and lots of people who just assumed that God was irrelevant and so their questions were really interesting. It really challenged me so I used to sit and read C. S. Lewis's *Mere Christianity* desperately at nights. I had a friend who had read lots of Richard Dawkins' books, so I read them too. I thought his theology was a bit off and he's just got a big chip on his shoulder but the books are really interesting. And so then I began to talk with my friend about why I thought Dawkins was wrong and one day the Principal of the college said to me, "Tamsin, why on earth are you a Christian?" And before I could answer my friend said, "Oh well I've been trying for the last three months to dissuade her and the truth is you can't prove there's no God." I asked my friend to read a book in return called *Who Moved the Stone?* by Frank Morison and he read the first page and then said he wasn't going to read any more because he might not be able to argue against it, and I found that really interesting because I'd always thought it's my fault that people don't see Jesus or it's my fault that people don't find God.

'I decided to join a church in Central London called St Paul's Onslow Square and that again was great because it was a good safe place where I knew I'd get good teaching and they pushed me into lots of leadership stuff straight off, such as leading small groups and helping on the Alpha Course. I got invited to go with other friends out to Latvia to help rebuild a church and to the Ukraine a few times, trying to partner churches in this country with churches in Ukraine as they emerged out of the Iron Curtain. It was an extraordinary privilege to meet people whose faith had been tested in ways that I could never imagine, whose families had been persecuted for their Christian faith. They had a quality of faith that was amazing.

'At the same time, after leaving art college, I worked freelance doing some photography and design and I worked as a decorator and then I ended up working in an internet company. I was doing a little bit of teaching in a prison that I'd managed to pick

up freelance and was beginning to wonder how all this fitted
together. It didn't seem like it was much of a career path. It was
probably teaching in prison that helped me get it most because I
loved it but what I loved more was talking to them about God.
We would end up having these amazing conversations, whilst I
would be busy counting all the gadgets that had to go back in
the cupboard that could be turned into weapons. It was partly
that that made me think, "Yeah, I don't really want to be an art
teacher. I actually want to help people discover that God loves
them, whoever they are."

'St Paul's Onslow Square was a part of Holy Trinity Brompton
[HTB] and I went along to one of their Focus holidays in 1997. I
was listening to David Pytches' talk one evening about his wife
and his ministry and about how he was very much putting his
wife first in terms of saying she was always the one that could
see where the Lord was taking them next. She was always the
one that could hear the Holy Spirit move and it was just very
honouring and I sat there and I thought, "Yeah, it's time to
go. It's time to do that thing called looking at whether I might
be called to ordination." I'd been thinking about it for quite a
while but I didn't dare say anything because I thought that if
I said something to someone then it might end up happening
automatically without me being able to say, "Actually, no, I've
changed my mind, I don't want to do this any more," and it
was very much listening to the way he talked. It was in an era
where it was still unusual for women to be ordained and in the
Evangelical Church lots of people were still wrestling with the
question of whether women can be in leadership but I don't ever
remember being told I couldn't be a leader as a woman.

'My dad's a vicar, my granddad's a vicar, my great-granddad's
a vicar, so really that was not going to be what I was going to do.
In fact when I was 14 I even made a vow that I wouldn't marry a
vicar and I wouldn't go to Bible college because I figured if you
didn't go to Bible college you couldn't become a vicar. But I did
like being in leadership and I did like making things happen. So
I made the decision to go and find out whether the Church of
England thinks this could be for me, whether God wants me to
be a vicar. I did do some quite in-depth Biblical work looking at
some of the passages that seemed to say women shouldn't lead

and I came to the conclusion that I couldn't see any reason why women shouldn't be leading, not least for the fact that there are umpteen women leaders in the Bible. My first step was to go to my vicar who was officially Sandy Miller at HTB and some people said he didn't like women to be vicars but we had a fantastic conversation. Part of me was still quite reluctant at this point anyway, so I was saying, "Oh I don't know what I want to be, I just know that this is the right step, I just think that this is what God wants me to do and who knows what I could do in the Church of England?" Because that's the amazing thing about the Church of England, there's so much you can do. It's not just about being a parish priest, that's the kind of bread and butter, but there are so many different roles.

'Sandy was really positive and put me forward and I saw the Director of Ordinands, a woman who couldn't have been more of a polar opposite to me. She was amazing, she was always beautifully turned out and I would turn up from work having cycled across town in my combats and my white t-shirt and I think she would despair of me because she was the epitome of cool. It was really good because she was quite testing, and asked me if I was doing this just because of my dad or my granddad. My brother was ordained as well by that stage. When I went to the selection conference she told me to sell myself more and to make sure they knew all the things I had done but when I met the senior selector he said, "Well I've read all your paperwork, do you think you might get bored in the Church of England?" I thought, "Oh OK so now we can have a conversation and I haven't got to try and tell you what I have been doing."

'In the end they said yes and I went to Wycliffe Hall in Oxford in 1998, a time when they were emerging into a good place about women. We built really good relationships there and listened to one another and learnt that some of the differences are about language and culture and not just theology. There were only five women in the first year and we were all quite loud and we made quite a big impact because we were gregarious and confident, and that changes how people relate to you. I met my husband Rob which was funny as of course I was never going to marry a vicar! When we got married I said, "I should have said that I'll never marry a very rich man and have a big house."

'Before we moved to London he was a rector of seven parishes in rural Gloucester while I was chaplain and he's now got a job at St Mellitus College. He's moved twice for me. After we left Oxford we decided that we wanted to job-share our curacy so that we would see each other and we ended up in a large church in Birmingham and it was quite amusing going back to my childhood haunts. I was the first woman taking communion and it was quite moving. Our family history there meant people trusted me even if they were conservative in opinion. In fact some of them gave me the biggest compliments in our time there, such as, "Your preaching is fantastic." And of course a woman preaching would be one of the key areas that they would have difficulty with and another one said to me, "Theologically I don't agree with women leaders but actually you've displayed great character." None of them were mean to me or unpleasant or got in my way or made life difficult. And whether it helped us being a couple coming into that and helping shift the ground a little, I don't know.

'Then a job got advertised at the University of Gloucestershire for a chaplain and Rob saw it and he thought that looked an amazing job for me. I phoned the Vice-Chancellor and asked what a university chaplain is meant to do in the twenty-first century. She said, "Be in the market place." And that was the bit that sold it because I'd loved being a curate in this big church, but I felt like people were always trying to pull me into the middle and actually I wanted to be out on the edges with people who didn't know what they thought or what they believed and to help them wrestle with that. I got the job and spent eight years there and loved it. I spent so much time with people who aren't in Church ever and I guess, partly because of my tradition as an evangelical, I'm not so worried about needing to have all the liturgical opportunities.

'For me, being evangelical is about taking the Bible seriously and not saying, "Oh because I don't like that bit I'm just going to ignore it." But equally, learning how to get the context and to understand what's being said, particularly over things like roles in marriage. I think for me that was a great example of cultural conditioning when we assume that because there is an order it has to be hierarchical when it is really about submitting by allowing someone else to flourish more. The Trinity is an interdependent relationship but with the Son submitting to the Father and the Spirit working with the Son and that's a model for all relationships. For me that's how to take scripture seriously whilst learning to understand it in my culture and working out how it applies in the Church. If as Christians you submit to Christ then it's meaningless who's in charge because Christ's the one in charge, so I think it's shaped within that, but it's definitely an understanding that in Genesis there's an order but it's not a hierarchy. I have had lots of conversations with some of the evangelists who hold a different opinion and I just have to disagree.

'I've met lots of Anglo-Catholics and Liberals who also have a sense of wanting to spread the gospel as an evangelist. I think Jesus is completely amazing and because I was the Chaplain people would ask questions or they'd want to know what Christians think, and I think one of the most heartbreaking things was meeting people who said, "I know that the Church hates people like me." It's heartbreaking because John's gospel said that God so loved the world that he gave his only son. I know it's complex and I know it's difficult sometimes if you say, "Actually, you know, morally we feel this is right and this is wrong," to then connect that to the person. So I think the other part of my job was about engaging with people and coming to understand how terrified most people were about walking into a chapel or talking to someone like me and how to learn to break down the barriers and drop a lot of the Christian jargon and make people comfortable. God is amazing and awe-inspiring but Christ was a man and he came to us as a man and we need both.

'After I'd done the job as chaplain for about seven years I missed the more regular community of a parish. I'd always been quite keen to come back to London and Rob was probably now in a place where he might be willing, but at that point he'd only been in his parish a short time. St Mary's advertised and so I thought I would have a look. It was a bit soon for Rob to leave but he said, "No, you need to do this because it's much tougher for women to be vicars and particularly in London so we need to put you first." I have been very fortunate in who

I've been married to. Rob came on the day of the interview to see the house and it looks really nice now but it didn't then and he did nearly die but they phoned up the same day to offer me the job through Rob because I was in the middle of nowhere in Malawi. I said yes and when we told his parishioners, they were so proud of the fact that I'd got this job and thought he should be behind me, which was very fortunate. It's a very modern issue if a couple both work as there's no guarantee you will both get a job together.

'I've got 21 nationalities in this Church, 60 per cent social housing and Islington is the fifth poorest borough in London with the second highest level of child poverty. Those are the headlines but actually the challenge here is getting St Mary's to believe in themselves. They don't even begin to grasp how amazing they are. Maybe that's a good thing but one of them has led a youth club for quite a few years and we did a Lent course, and as part of that we were looking at what is mission and what is mercy. Rather than making it about the missionaries that go to Africa, she sat there and went, "So is my youth club mission?" It works with kids who don't go to Church so of course it is. Now there's a passion coming because she's getting the "why" and understanding that actually it's not necessarily about making them come to Church but it's about her own witness.

'It's amazing how quite senior people in a church can dismiss their contribution because it's not tangible and yet how crucial they are. It's getting people to see that they can invite their friends into the Church and the target is not whether they come but can you invite them as a person who loves Christ and represents the Church. They can always say no, and that's OK, but sometimes they like to be invited. One of the things I want to develop actually comes out of the funerals I do, thinking about how we do the follow-up and carry on building relationships even if they never come to church. People need hope and I think that's what I love doing more than anything – saying to people there's hope. One of the advantages of being a woman, for example, is at a funeral. You can hug people and you can give them a kiss and it's not that men can't do that but it's much easier as a woman. I'd had to do a funeral of a stillborn baby and the lady who works at the burial chapel was saying to me,

"I think it's great when it's a woman because you can give the mum a hug and a kiss", although I would say my husband's far more empathetic than me.

'There's a pressure here in the city. London is a place where there's a lot of talk about growth but it's not in a way that makes you feel bad. There's a great understanding that if you're doing local Church that really is trying to reach out and that's relational then it's a good thing. On one level there's a pressure to see the money but on another there's also an understanding in the places that are the poorest that half your congregation may be without a job.'

I first heard of Tamsin in connection with the conference she was running to encourage women into the Church. As she often points out, the Evangelical Church has not always been the best at encouraging women and some more conservative parts of the Church have been completely against their ordination. This is particularly frustrating when they are often the churches seeing the greatest growth, particularly with younger people. I have met a number of young women who would make wonderful priests but they had not felt it was a possibility. They had failed to see good role models and were not getting any encouragement from their leaders. Tamsin was right to be taking a lead on this and she explained more about her interest.

'I have got involved in a conference for young women because it's exciting that the Ministry Division have been encouraging vocations under 30 in the Church. For every seven young men there were only two women coming forward and in the Evangelical or Anglo-Catholic Churches it would be even lower. As I looked into it I realised how important I thought it was and we wanted to provide a safe place where you can say, "Is God calling me?" and to look at some of the issues in an informal way. And we recognise that there are some specific issues to being evangelical. We need young people in the Church because young people see the world differently and have all the energy. On the one hand we have a culture which lauds the young and wants to do more for them but on the other hand I think we also have a culture that slightly looks down on what young people can genuinely contribute. We want a Church where people will give the best of their life to the Church.

'We know from some research that women tend to look at a role and look at all the things they can't do or if there's a list and they can't do 50 per cent of it then they say, "Well that's not for me because I can't do those things." A man will look at the role and see the 50 per cent they can do and go, "I'll blag the rest." In the younger age group, men tend to have greater confidence in themselves and the role models tend to be men, particularly in evangelical Churches. Women might be leading but not be ordained. We've been asking vicars to deliberately look at finding young women in their Church who they think may have a calling and ask them because we feel that women may need to be asked more than men and may need to be pushed a little bit more. If we believe in the Church of England – and I do think it is amazing – then we want to find the best as well and if we're going to have women bishops then we want to have the best women to choose from.

'I've been involved in the debate on women bishops mostly in conversation with conservative leaders about their concerns. I think that the legislation needs to be incredibly simple. I understand why people have been asking for something that's more complex but I think that then undermines what the woman is as a bishop. It's difficult when you know why people don't want something and you can see that some of what they're saying is out of fear and some of that's from the experience of feeling shut down in certain areas. Women bishops are essential because, for me, if I go back to Genesis, God made man and woman in his image and he made them to be in partnership with him and I don't see anything that tells me that they shouldn't be involved. The Gospel is the good news of the Kingdom of God and the Kingdom of God is bringing in a time of no suffering and no tears and it's about there being "no longer Jew or Greek ... slave or free ... male and female" (Gal. 3.28). For me the Kingdom of God is a place where people are called into their role because God called them, so if someone can't do that role because they say, "You can't do that role," then I would say it's thwarting the Kingdom of God. I think certainly as a witness to issues of injustice it doesn't help when the Church can't work itself out.'

Tamsin has an incredibly busy life, like many working women, and I wondered how she managed to find any kind of balance. Many vicars find themselves seriously over-worked, dealing with the demands of parish life in all it's different forms from Sunday services and other types of worship to ceremonial occasions and administration. A vicar in the Church of England also has a particular role to care for everyone in the parish, whether they come to church or not, which adds to the demands on them.

'Getting balance in my life happens both with difficulty and with ease. On the one hand I think understanding what drives you helps, so I know for me one of the things that drives me comes from when I was at school and the reports said, "You could do better." I hated school so I really could have done better, but actually now I would want to ask my teachers if they could have done a bit better. I know I have to be careful of that little mantra and work out when I have done enough. I think the other is having things that I enjoy doing, so I think if you don't have anything that you want to go and do then you're not going to go and have a life. I love being in London and getting on the bus and going to the galleries for free. Rob and I do now share a day off which is good and helps us get some work-life balance. Ironically I've moved to London from the countryside and I now listen to *The Archers* and have even begun gardening. I'm also quite good at saying, "I am not doing anything for an hour. I am going to sit in a heap and read a book."'

Favourite verse: 2 Corinthians 4.18 'Because we look not at what can be seen but at what cannot be seen; for what can be seen is temporary, but what cannot be seen is eternal.'

Favourite woman: Deborah in the Book of Judges because it says she was the Judge over all Israel at the time and it doesn't say, 'because there were no men to do the job'. I also like her because she wants her male commander to go into battle but he's a bit of a sissy and says in Judges 4.8, 'If you will not go with me, I will not go', so she tells him that she will go but the glory will then go to a woman instead and the enemy will die at the hands of a woman. I like her because she's the only female Judge and she's willing to go into battle which is what they had to do and she wouldn't take any namby-pamby nonsense.

6

Dr Elaine Storkey

Elaine Storkey is a well-known theologian, broadcaster and writer who has brought a Biblical perspective to the feminist movement. She was listed as one of the top 100 female public intellectuals in the *Guardian* and sees herself as a 'liberated evangelical' although she prefers not to bother with such labels. Her career includes roles as Executive Director of the London Institute of Contemporary Christianity, senior research fellow at Wycliffe Hall, Oxford and Director of Training for the Church Army, as well as President of the Christian international relief and development charity Tearfund.

I have always admired her willingness to fight many kinds of injustice but her particular gift has been to speak up for women. She spoke on behalf of women deacons in the debates in the 1990s before the vote on women priests, as she felt strongly that their voices needed to be heard. As President of Tearfund she spent 16 years travelling the world highlighting numerous issues that particularly affect the poor, from climate change to violence against women. Her 20 years of broadcasting for *Thought for the Day* on Radio 4 gave her a significant platform to encourage women and no doubt irritate some of the male listeners.

I visited her and her husband Alan at their house in a village near Cambridge and found her very warm and humorous, particularly for someone who focuses on rather serious and difficult subjects. I was soon to learn that a great sense of humour is a key part of her personality and it has made her many visits to Tearfund projects even more memorable for those involved. She had a very happy childhood in Yorkshire as the child of intellectually ambitious parents who had their own education cut short. Elaine enjoyed school and loved the academic side and feels this upbringing defined her life. She went on to the University of Wales, Aberystwyth to study philosophy, but I was curious to know how she became a Christian and ultimately a feminist theologian and whether she had ever considered being ordained.

'I became a Christian when I was 16, largely through the Methodist Church. I was an Anglican by background but the Methodists were much more vibrant. I was taken to a youth gathering, heard the Gospel and responded and I thought that was it. However, although I went up to university as a Christian, my faith was pretty much shattered by the beginning of the second year. This was partly because it was very flimsy, it wasn't based on anything particularly thought-through or strong. I knew the scriptures very well by then but what I couldn't do was to relate it cogently to some of the big issues that were coming up all the time in my philosophy course. So I went through a dark night of the soul in my second year, where for a period of about six weeks I didn't believe anything or anybody. And it felt like looking over the abyss, there was a great void there and nothing made sense and therefore nothing had any meaning. I found out afterwards that the philosophy tutor was a firm atheist and thought it was great sport to have this Christian in his class. He had set himself out to demolish my faith and was playing all kinds of games as well and I wasn't up to it. I was very young and there were no Christians who could help. They could pray for you but they hadn't a clue what I was really worrying about.

'Curiously what brought me out of that time was the Christian women who came to my room to tuck me in and pray for me and one night one of them said, "I think you're going to be alright." And I said, "Please leave me, just shut the lights off as you go." And they went and I shouted again, "Please put the light off." And I looked up and there was nobody in the room but there was a light there. Extraordinary. And I had what I can only describe as a very deep experience of God and peace. The light faded and I went to sleep and the next morning I felt completely different. I had no idea what it was, it just felt good. It was something to do with the fact that these girls had just been praying for me and it was peaceful. I felt better, physically and mentally, and decided to go back to lectures, to the same lecturer who'd demolished my thinking. And I just heard him for the first time, really heard him and heard the assumptions he was making. And I just thought what a fool I was to be swayed by this and I went back into the fray.

'I think that period was important for me because I can still remember it quite clearly. It was a time firstly where I began to understand what thoughtful non-Christians go through, people who really care about meaning and truth and the point of it all. I mean, it must be hell for a lot of them. And, secondly, I realised that there are people out there who would destroy us, it's a sport to them and you don't actually give them much leeway. And, thirdly, it's about trying to stand alongside doubters, people who want to believe in God, desperately want to believe but can't for whatever reason. So those have been the three important planks for my life.

'However, it never occurred to me to be ordained as in those days women who were ordained became deaconesses. And I couldn't work out whether they were honorary clergy wives or parish doormats, because they seemed so uninteresting. I was very disparaging towards deaconesses and I felt sorry for the ones I met as they seemed to have no kind of life. Nuns were much more interesting because they had a level of autonomy. So there was nothing at all about ordination that interested me and I think I was always going to be an academic. Later on, when I actually was an academic and speaking on behalf of women who were called to be priests, then I saw the attraction. And of course since then I have moved into a priestly role myself in a whole range of ways and find this quite natural. And it was suggested about 15 years ago that now is the time to be ordained and I thought through it a lot and still decided that I'm best as a lay woman doing the kind of things I do. I started my career as a philosophy tutor at Manchester College, Oxford and then I married Alan and followed him to Stirling University. I became a theologian through the work I did rather than going back to study it.

'I hadn't thought about feminism at all as a young woman because I didn't really have any restraints. As an academic woman I did what I wanted. I was usually the only woman in the department but that never seemed odd. It was just what you put up with. When I had my first son, Alan and I were co-parenting and he was working from home, but then he went out to work and it knocked me for six. I had the choice of going out to work too and I was pregnant with my second child by then and thinking, "No, I don't want to, I actually want to stay at home with these two tinies because they're really interesting, far more interesting than adults." But by the time my second son was born and I was literally at home on my own and Alan was at college, I didn't know what to do. I would phone women up and say, "This is going to sound a really daft question but what do you do all day?" And they would say, "We do the housework" and I said, "No, I've done the housework." They said, "You can't have done it, it's only 11 o'clock in the morning" and I just thought, "This is a bit bizarre."

'So I threw myself into bringing my kids up as an academic. We taught them to read and do maths and square roots and we had labels on everything so they were reading by the time they were two-and-a-half or three. It was ridiculous but it's what I did. I also did a lot of writing but, when my youngest was born and Alan had gone out to work, I felt I had to do something more so I trotted down to the local Further Education College and asked to teach night classes to housebound women like myself. I offered Sociology and Philosophy at O and A level and it was fabulous. I realised, when teaching these women, how the limitations on their lives were enormous, absolutely colossal. At any stage, I could have just upped and got a much more interesting full-time job and put my kids in a nursery but they didn't have those facilities. Their lives were very restricted. As a result I became very interested in feminism and started reading all the feminist literature. But my feeling then was the way out was for these women to become Christians. If you put them in touch with God then they would find their own identity, as I had, in Christ and they would know who they were and then the limitations wouldn't matter so much or they would be rescheduled in some kind of way. So I became really desperate to engage these women.

'When I say I wanted to help women to find their own identity, it was mostly sitting down and listening, trying to work out what made these women tick, what their hopes and ambitions were, how they saw life, what their fears were, what was their biggest worry. And a lot of them were actually worried about unfaithfulness. Women would say things to me like, "Well you never really know if your husband's having an affair do you?" And I would find that staggering, the whole idea that you couldn't trust your partner. And a lot of people were drifting in and out of relationships and were looking for a relationship that would give them what they felt they needed. So it was about trying to engage with that. There were loads of opportunities as a Christian, not just to be judgemental but to actually give a bigger perspective on life and a bigger shape to morality and relationships and forgiveness.

'I also wanted to help women to recognise what their calling is, what their gifts are, what God has given them. They're not always the up-front kind of gifts that we take from a male type model. They can be very different gifts of leadership and there's something wonderful about the kind of servant leadership that ought to be operating everywhere. Being a woman who enjoys hospitality and being in the background is still a form of leadership. It's creating the kind of atmosphere and the kind of peace and space where people can be themselves and therefore can hear God better in those situations and they can share. I'd like to have had the gift of hospitality more than that of teaching because it's a warmer gift, it's a more peaceful gift, whereas teaching is jolly hard work. The problem now is that there are people who have other gifts such as being a bishop but they can't. We don't have the same rules for men and women.

'Eventually I became an Open University tutor and stayed with them for 15 years or more, finally becoming a full-time lecturer. I was doing Social Sciences and was the only Christian in a predominantly Marxist department. I wrote a book called *What's Right with Feminism* which looked at the history of feminism and the reasons why the feminist agenda is a really significant one, whether you're looking at the home, domestic relationships, work, professions, education, health or even the law. After that, life became really bizarre and I started doing lots of radio broadcasting including *Thought for the Day*. I was speaking at conferences everywhere and writing on different subjects for the Church of England. I became involved in many different organisations but the interesting thing is I hardly ever applied for a job, they were just offered to me.'

Elaine was eventually asked by the hugely influential Christian leader John Stott to run the evangelical London Institute of Contemporary Christianity. This was a big change from working as a Christian feminist in a secular context and she found it slightly constraining, although any negative issues for her as a woman were always with the Church and the people outside the Institute. She recalled an earlier incident when she had been the only woman teaching at Oak Hill theological college alongside her Open University work.

'The Principal was wonderful as were most of the staff but there were a couple of staff members who were really dreadful and there weren't any women students at that stage either so they would play silly games. I remember when a rather portly bishop came to the front door. He saw me, thought "Oh a woman, secretary, slave" and said "My dear, be a good girl will you and make me a cup of tea and would you pop into the Principal and let him know that Bishop so and so has arrived?" So I said to him, "Do you know, I would if I could but I'm just on my way to deliver a philosophy lecture but if you go down there you'll find a kettle and if you go round the corner you'll find the Principal's secretary and she will help you." Well this story went round Oak Hill that I'd told a Bishop to go and make himself a cup of tea and the Principal thought it was very funny. But that just struck me as extraordinary. Woman doesn't mean "equal" or "academic" or "educator" or "priest", it just means "my servant". So you've got the whole flavour of that in the Church and some of the young men were quite full of themselves too. I found the anti-women theology was a bit much.

'Women have been patronised by the Church for yonks really. I remember when my children were very small, at a Mother's Day service, some poor curate brought this wretched cardboard cut-out of a woman and put it in the centre of the Church and got all the kids to the front and said, "Now what do our mothers do for us?" And I looked with horror at the kind of props he'd got: dishcloths, tea towels, aprons and nappies. And the kids had to say something that their mother did for them and then pin it on. And I was thinking this could be terrible when it comes to my youngest son Caleb's turn. So he said, "Caleb, what does your mother do?" "She teaches philosophy", said Caleb and he had nothing to pin on and the curate was disgusted with my son. He was outraged. Just typical of the patronising way that we approach women in the Church.'

Elaine has been the President of Tearfund since 1997, visiting projects all over the world and helping communicate the Church's calling to tackle poverty and speak up for justice. She brings valuable theological insight to many difficult issues and her wisdom has inspired many staff and supporters. As a trustee of Tearfund I have been lucky to hear her speak about Tearfund's crucial role as a Christian organisation in lifting people out of both material and spiritual poverty. She also helped set up an organisation called Restored, an international Christian alliance working to transform relationships and end violence against women. She was keen to tell me more about her role and her specific interest in abused women.

'When I was asked to become President I thought, "I can't do this when there are people out there who have given their lives to Tearfund and I've done almost nothing so it would be presumptuous of me to become its President." But I was phoned up by the Chairman of the Board who said, "Elaine, we know that, we've got all the records, all the donation records, we think you've been useless but we're giving you a chance to make amends!" Isn't that lovely? In 2001 I was asked to go to Haiti because they needed a French speaker and an education-alist, as they were going to be monitoring all of these schools. So I went and it completely changed my whole horizon as I was actually living with people who were struggling with poverty. I was visiting small Christian schools up and down the country, looking at our partners and the work they were doing but also looking at the way in which women's lives were really limited. The vocational schools were run on very traditional lines where women were taught to sew and knit and the boys were given engineering and electronic projects. But that's what Haiti needed, that's what the women needed.

'I also went to Africa with Tearfund and I love the way they work, the whole idea of letting people think through their own resources and then mapping out their own needs and what they've got to meet those needs and then facilitating that rather than telling them how to do it. It's such an integrated programme as you can't tackle poverty without tackling education, without tackling HIV/AIDS, without tackling women, without tackling empowerment. And suddenly, before you know where you are, when you're mapping out your needs, you realise just how much you need and how much women need and that challenges all your stereotypes.

'And we found that the ones that had been doing this particular project for ten years were really not poor any more. And what's more, they had better relationships, they had a much stronger grasp on how to produce things for markets and how to educate their kids. And leadership patterns were fairly developed. But the communities just starting out had difficult issues and a lot of these were around gender. Every time I go on a Tearfund trip I ask if I can speak to women on their own as that is the only way to get an authentic voice.

'The specific issue of domestic violence came out on my first trip to the Congo in 2006. I've always known about violence and I was already bothered about some of the practices that happen to women but that trip knocked me for six. Going down the whole of the Kivu province and through the camps was really horrendous. A Tearfund partner called Heal Africa was serving the victims of the war but, realising that they were doing nothing for the women who had been raped and seriously damaged, they began this process, putting up a notice to say that any woman who wanted to have counselling or help from the hospital with sexual violence should please present themselves this morning. They had a long prayer meeting early that morning and at 7 o'clock they could hear the women coming and at 7.30 they could smell them. They had 200 women before they had to shut the doors because they just couldn't take any more. And a lot of them needed fistula operations and had quite damaged bodies needing other surgery. When I went there I visited the women who were still there recovering from operations, two to a bed. And their stories … I almost couldn't take any more. Stories of little girls being gang-raped and girls who had been blinded so that they would never identify their attacker. And girls who had been maimed and children who had had their mothers raped in front of them and their sisters bayoneted. It was absolutely brutal and ghastly, it was really horrible. What hit me was that the people doing something about it were the Christians, and I was profoundly grateful for that. And the Christian guys as well, they really shone.

'At the last place we visited I was leading Bible studies for the team that morning. And I thought, "I've really got to do something on gender because we can't sweep it under the carpet, we can't just regard it as normal, we've got to have it up front." So we did an exposition of the passage on the woman who anointed Jesus in Luke 7 and then I challenged them. I asked them whether their gender attitudes were African cultural attitudes or Christian attitudes, because the two were not necessarily the same. I tried to unpack how cultural attitudes change and Biblical attitudes are very rooted in their identity as persons and in our relationship with God and they have to shape our culture but we can let some things go, culturally. And I pointed out how in the UK culture shifted all the time and what men did in one generation they didn't do in another. So the way that my father brought me up was quite different from the way that my husband had brought our sons up and very different from the way that our sons brought their children up. And I gave examples, telling them that my sons would help feed their children and wash their clothes and collect them from school, all normal things women used to do. And I looked around and all these guys looked at me as if I'd just dropped off Mars and I realised I had made some kind of impact.

'Well the next morning the leader of the compound met me and said, "I haven't slept all night, I've been worrying about what you said yesterday morning. Did I hear you say your sons wash their children's clothes?" So I said, "Well, they put them in the washing machine. No big deal but they take the responsibility for that." So he said, "Well that's what kept me awake all night. I kept saying to myself, would I wash my children's clothes and I thought no, I would not. Why wouldn't I? And the reason I wouldn't is because it would be demeaning for me as a man to do a woman's work. And then God said to me, "and what does that mean about your attitude to women, who do you think you are?"' And he said it kept him awake all night and it really,

really worried him. And we just had to pray there and then. He just had an epiphany. And not only did we pray, he went round all the churches in the area and asked the male church elders to meet me and let me preach at their churches and so on. I had a very busy week. I suddenly realised that those people who love the scriptures and love the word of God and actually are open to the Holy Spirit can be transformed and have their attitudes changed. I found that very encouraging, even in the darkest places. It's not a kind of moral blackmail, it's just people being willing to open themselves up to a new perspective.

'Gender issues have always been part of Tearfund's brief but we hadn't fully taken on the whole issue of violence to women and that's why I helped set up Restored as an embryonic organisation within Tearfund. I think it's making a big difference. Restored has really started to challenge structures, it's started to work with men. The programme of First Man Standing is brilliant, calling men to respect women, challenge other men and speak out against violence against women. I think it's wonderful that a man is leading it, as he can speak to men in a way that women can't.

'In terms of speaking out on social justice issues in the Church as a whole, at one level it is to do with the fact that women's voices haven't been heard in the Church. But at the second level, it's that the voices that have been heard are the women who have been seen as professional career women within the Church. And so the focus of the Church's attitude and relationship with women has largely been, "What do we do with the women in our Church? Do we let them become priests and bishops and so on?" And that has often clouded the bigger issue of what do we do about men and women working together in the Church, both in terms of colleagues as priests and bishops but just as important, if not more important, in the home, as husbands and wives, as fathers and mothers? And as those who are respecting each other in the whole range of activities and work. And that's got missed, it's just got sidetracked. We're the European capital for teenage pregnancy and yet what are we doing in churches about that? How are we helping our teenage girls to cope with the culture that's out there and to protect them and give them a sense of identity but also to let them know that intimacy is about something deeper? There are horrifying studies out there on teenage violence, even suggesting that violence is part of intimacy now. It can be the price a girl has to pay for having a boyfriend. Why are we not really addressing that in our preaching and in practical ways?

'There are some Church leaders who care enormously about these things and you can see when we put on particular fringe meetings at Synod that it's a priority for some but it's not everyone. I'm sure a lot of it's a lack of awareness, they don't realise how big the problem is. I think some of it is a sense that, "Well this is the way the world is. That's why we've got to evangelise. And so the answer is evangelism." And the answer is evangelism at one level but when you've evangelised and somebody hears the Gospel, the next question is, "What then? How do you live this out?" And so it's the whole purpose of living out the Gospel that we seem to be very poor on. We need to frame something that's publicly visible as an alternative to the mess that our culture has got itself into. In every parish we should be working with people who are moving into relation-ships but not getting married, for example. But what's the Church doing? We're missing huge opportunities to work with those people on relationships and to fan those relationships into deep commitments and marriage.

'There's also a fear that's in many people's own families. I've had women tell me, "My daughter's in this position, what do I do? If I'm judgemental then I lose my daughter." It's steering the line of actually holding a doctrinal position firmly but being pastorally sensitive and open and loving so that you're saying, "This is where I stand but I still want to embrace where you are and I want to help you as much as I can." And I think a lot of parents feel defeated, the culture is too big for them and it's savage out there. A lot of people stand by and watch their kids go through terrible times and don't really know what to do. It's hard.

'I do see the Church in some of the countries and the commu-nities that I visit as a harbinger of hope and far from being the problem but I think the Church is the problem in the UK. I think the Church's own attitudes towards gender and women have constituted a bigger issue for people out there than the healing and the love that we should be offering. It's not the case in parts of Africa. The Mothers' Union, for example, is incredible in Africa and organises groups to protect schoolgirls from rape. It takes all of these things terribly seriously. And I think the same is true even in India. At the moment there's a huge battle in India against selective abortion, which is ridiculously high but it's Christian voices as well as other voices that are speaking out in these areas. So I wouldn't blame the Church for a lot of these things, although I think that the Church in Africa is a very patriarchal church and they've got to get their own house sorted out in these areas, but there are also areas where Christians are working like mad to alleviate the problems.'

Elaine did not seem to play a particularly prominent role in the recent debate on women bishops until it came to the issue of an amendment to allow separate episcopal oversight for those against women bishops. At that point she argued that whilst people should not be penalised for their convictions there should not be a clause that reinforces separatism within the Church. It would undermine the authority of women bishops and she couldn't support it. I was interested to get her theological insights, both as an academic and as an evangelical.

'When it comes to the issue of women bishops what I'm mostly doing is answering people who think that there shouldn't be women in that role rather than actually speaking out because to me it's a no-brainer, it's terribly evident. People who are against are usually coming from two specific viewpoints. One is what's now called "complimentarianism", which is a hierarchical view about male headship and about the order of creation and so on. The other is a sacramental position that says priests have to be icons of Christ, which means they have to look like Christ in some way or another and therefore the gender gets subsumed under that. I want to say they are both half-baked positions but that sounds too insulting. I think they both miss the point in a whole range of ways.

'As an evangelical woman you've got to take seriously what the scriptures say but not just nitpick the odd passage from Timothy or Corinthians. You've got to see the whole sweep of Biblical literature right from the beginning with Genesis through to Revelation. And when you look at it very carefully and get the map from the scripture itself rather than from the map that we're putting on scripture, I think very different patterns come out.

'You can't anchor the debate down just to the concept of difference, which is really what most of the opponents want to do, that men and women are different, they have different roles, different callings, different theology, different spirituality and therefore we find them roles and the jobs for them to do that celebrate those differences. Fine, men and women are different, that's a very strong scriptural precedent. It's there all the way through the Bible but men and women are also the same and that's a theme that goes right through scripture. We are not just similar but we're the same in terms of human creation, man and woman are in union in that sense. We're the same in terms of our sin and we both need God's redemption and forgiveness. We're the same in terms of our gifting, you find incredibly gifted women in the Old Testament who become Prophets and become Judges and lead nations. And that is odd when you consider what a patriarchal nation Israel was, but the fact that you have these women and they are there in scripture for us is key. And we're the same in our need for forgiveness, in our need for Christ and as image bearers and we're the same in our gifting. There are many women in the New Testament who've got prophetic and teaching gifts.

'So I think that the four concepts for me are difference and similarity held together and then complimentarity where we fit together because we need each other and the main concept is union: that men and women are always in union as the image of Christ or as the body or bride of Christ. And that union means that we have to find ways of working together. And I think that's a much better theology because it takes seriously all the Bible is saying rather than the theology of difference, which just nitpicks, takes one or two bits and ignores the rest. The issue of male dominance doesn't come in the creation story, it comes in the sin story when the curse happens and men and women are given different roles. Of course we worry about the sin passages but when you come to Christ you get a very full picture of the redemption story which bears almost no relationship to the brokenness and inhumanity that comes before. So if you put the rape of the concubine in Judges 19 alongside Jesus' treatment of the Samaritan woman at the well in John 4, they are eons apart. Christ is showing us the redemptive nature of the Gospel. The focus for me is always on Jesus and his relationship with women because he too was part of his culture and he breaks the culture in umpteen different ways, the culture that is so restrictive to women, whether they're menstruating [seen as ritually unclean] or divorced women or whatever else. Jesus just walks right through it.'

That final remark from Elaine about the relationship Jesus has with women is, for me, the core of the issue about the role of women, making it impossible for me to accept the theological arguments that have caused such anguish to so many women across the world, whether in Churches in the West or villages in Africa. Elaine has used her gifts as a speaker and writer to articulate clearly and simply many of the issues that have caused such pain. Her love for women and her passion for justice shines through everything she does. Her role in Tearfund has been inspirational and ensured that the growing abuse of women is increasingly understood and that more and more women are getting help and support.

She has always had a practical approach to theology and an extraordinary ability to communicate. In 1989 she wrote a short book called *Losing a Child* following the death of a baby girl belonging to close friends. She had looked after the baby the night before she died and it made her aware of the awful fear that lives with you, that you might lose your child or grandchild. It had a big response and as she says, 'What is the Christian perspective on losing a child? At the end of the day we don't know why life is so cruel to some people, we don't know why life is so broken, but we do know that God knows and we do know that God is there with us. And we also know that that child's life was not a waste and I think that's very important for people. Alan's cousin had a child who wasn't due to live but survived for nine months and at the child's funeral his father said, "Christopher's brought more people to Christ during the nine months of his life than I have during the 35 years of mine." The relationship between the parents and the child they loved so deeply was so transparently Christian and so full of Christian hope, it did communicate.'

Favourite verse: Colossians 1:15 'He [Christ] is the image of the invisible God, the firstborn of all creation.'

Favourite woman: I absolutely love the story of the bleeding [menstruating] woman who touches Jesus in Luke 8.40–8. I've sat through so many sermons on this and they always miss the point. The reason that she doesn't own up to him and say, 'Yes, I touched you', is not because she's naturally modest, it's because she's just defiled a Jewish rabbi by touching him when she is officially 'unclean' and he's now got to go home and change all his clothes with ritual ablutions and so on. And he doesn't, he just gives her peace and says, "Your faith has made you well." He calls her 'daughter' because she's the daughter of Abraham and it's reaffirming her Jewishness and the fact that she's actually violated the law but she's a daughter of Abraham. It's a powerful story and I love her gutsiness, determination and faith.

7

Dr Jane Williams

Jane Williams is a gifted and successful theologian, teacher, freelance writer and editor. She is married to Dr Rowan Williams, previously Archbishop of Canterbury and, following his appointment as a Life Peer in the House of Lords, she now has the full title of Lady Williams of Oystermouth. His new role as Master of Magdalene College in Cambridge means that Jane divides her time between Cambridge and London, where her son is still at school. She teaches at St Mellitus College and is a visiting lecturer at King's College, London. She has published a number of books and was recently awarded an honorary doctorate at Yale University, partly for her work 'in promoting and encouraging the role of women in the Anglican Communion'.

Although I was interested in Jane's own views on women in the Church, I thought it might be hard for her to be completely objective when she had been so close to the situation in her home life. It would be understandable if she was defensive about her husband as she would have shared in the pain caused by so much criticism from all sides of the debate. He was known to have been supportive of women bishops but his very obvious determination to keep unity throughout the Anglican Communion made the situation more difficult and some would say it led to the failure of the final vote in 2012.

For many, Rowan Williams is a remarkable man who modelled a very Christ-like and humble style of leadership and accomplished a great deal, particularly internationally. Canon Andrew White, the well-known vicar of Baghdad, describes him as a 'true living saint, scholar and servant of God'. Rowan said many important things about society, economics and the role of the Church but these were often misinterpreted by the media, leading to criticism for a lack of robust leadership and a

real strategy for the Church. I imagine that kind of misinterpre-
tation would have been hard for any wife to accept but could
see that she would have been a wonderful support through
difficult times.

We met at their new home at Magdalene, a surprisingly
modern building situated in the grounds of the fifteenth-century
college but also well suited to the entertaining that is required
in this role. Jane is a petite, gentle and softly spoken woman but
she is clearly tougher than she looks and has a delightful sense
of humour that must have helped her through some challenging
moments. Rowan has described her father Geoffrey Paul (Bishop
of Hull and later Bradford) as 'one of the greatest Christians I
have been privileged to know', so I was keen to know more
about her childhood and her decision to be an academic rather
than choosing to be ordained.

'I grew up in South India. My parents were missionaries there
for the Church Mission Society and I was born there and lived
there until I was about eight. I'm one of five sisters, so it was
like a Jane Austen family and I think I've always assumed that
the world was largely feminine. Although my father was a very
strong personality, it was an overwhelmingly female household.
I went to a girls' boarding school in the hills so I never really
had that feeling of either competition or inferiority to men as I
was growing up. But it was quite a shock when I came to read
theology at Clare College, Cambridge.

'Being a Christian and growing up in a Christian family was
and is a really important part of my life and kept me going
through some very tough times at boarding school because
God was the bit of the family that came with you wherever you
went. I was very much aware that God was part of our family
culture for me and I wanted to find out whether that's all it
was or whether I actually believed in God myself. I think that's
why I decided to study theology. I thought if I gave it a kind of
rigorous going-over I would find out if I still believed it at the
end. I found I did and I realised that a big part of my spirituality is the intellectual excitement of God. Studying theology has
never been a distraction for me. I realise that isn't the same for
everybody but for me it has really deepened my faith to explore
it like that and I do strongly believe that if a faith can't be

examined then it can't be a real faith; if you think God is going to disappear if you ask difficult questions about Him then that's not a God worth having.

'Of course it is just faith and in the end there isn't a logical argument that proves the existence of God and I would want to argue that that says something about the nature of the God I believe in. If you could prove the existence of God then we wouldn't have any choice about believing in God, and the Christian faith has always said that God leaves us free to relate or not to relate. So the fact that there are going to be unanswered questions is part of the nature of God. But I also think that either God is truth or God isn't truth and if God is truth then there is no truth that God is afraid of and that we do need some Christians who are not afraid to ask questions and to come up against blank walls occasionally. I don't think that's everybody's calling but it's exciting for me.

'It was quite unusual to be a woman in Cambridge when I was a student here. I suppose I hadn't ever realised before that men had brains. Even my father didn't really count because he was my father. For me to realise that men are complex human beings and have feelings and emotions and thoughts just the same as women do was really quite an eye-opener, and quite an intriguing insight into how it's possible in a very male culture for men not to know that about women. It's quite interesting that I came at it the other way round. I was the only theologian in my year at Clare, which meant that most of my friends were doing other subjects and I discovered really early on that when people are a little bit drunk in the middle of the night they want to talk about God if there's somebody there that they identify with the subject. Certainly a lot of our children's friends really want to talk to Rowan about God late at night even now.

'I met Rowan when I was doing my doctoral research in Cambridge and we got married shortly after that, when he was a curate there. What I did to earn a living at that point was to work for Cambridge University Press as a freelance sub-editor, which was great fun and gave me an opportunity to go on reading things that I wouldn't otherwise have done. And then we moved to Oxford where I didn't work for a bit. Rowan was the Lady Margaret Professor of Divinity and a canon of Christ

Church. And that's where we had our first child [a daughter] so for a few years I was working very hard as a wife and mother. I kept reading and did little bits of writing and some freelance teaching and editing to fit around the family.

'After Oxford, Rowan became Bishop of Monmouth and then Archbishop of Wales, so we were there for ten years and expected to stay there, to be truthful. There was a very strong sense of being called home to Wales for Rowan and all through his life he's combined the academic and the pastoral, he's never wanted to do just one or the other. So in Oxford it was largely academic and in Monmouth obviously it was largely church-based and pastoral but with a clear teaching gift that he has been able to use.

'I've never felt that I played a supportive role in Rowan's ministry, if I'm honest. I know a lot of people see it as a joint calling and I recognise that's right for them but it's not how we ever felt about it but I hope I was always supportive of him. Obviously our home was like any other clergy home, very full of people, and that bit I loved. But I don't think I have ever been a typical bishop's wife and I don't think I've met a typical bishop's wife. A great majority of them have at least a part-time job and some are ordained themselves, which will be an interesting one to work through. You can lose a bit of your voice as a bishop's wife but you also gain quite a bit of voice and have extraordinary privileges.

'In terms of any calling of my own, I think if you'd asked me when I was 18 I would simply have assumed I was going to get ordained but without really having any clear sense of calling or why I made that assumption. It seemed like the family business, but in reality it just wasn't a possibility at that time and the women that I saw being deaconesses, well some of them were absolutely wonderful but they didn't look like a really attractive role model for an 18-year-old. And then, as time went on, when people ask me why I'm not ordained I just say, "Well God never asked me." And as somebody who's worked in theological education and with potential ordinands all my life I think that sense of being called to it is absolutely vital.'

Although Jane chose not to be ordained she plays a very significant role in the life of many potential ordinands by teaching at St Mellitus College, one of the largest and most innovative places to study theology and ministry in the UK. St Mellitus was founded in London in 2007 by the Bishops of London and Chelmsford and was the result of two institutions coming together. One of these was St Paul's Theological Centre which had grown out of Holy Trinity Brompton. Known as HTB, this well-known and influential evangelical Church has had a huge impact not only by planting other Churches but also as the home of the Alpha Course. Like many people I had made some false assumptions about the attitude to women of the Evangelical Church and was keen to understand more about attitudes to women in such an influential place.

'In 2005 I started teaching doctrine and systematics at St Paul's [now St Mellitus] which I love. We are training people across the whole spectrum of age and orthodoxy within the Church. When Nicky Gumbel [vicar of HTB] and Graham Tomlin [now Dean of St Mellitus] were thinking of starting this new form of training they were looking around for people who had theological education backgrounds and could help with the setting up of it. I had grown up in the evangelical tradition and had been formed by the charismatic tradition as well and Rowan had worked closely with Alpha in Wales, so we had good connections there. I said yes but I wasn't sure there would be enough ordinands who would want to train in that kind of way, which shows how wrong you can be. I just get this sense of God hanging about tapping his toes until we got the point.

'At the St Paul's end there are still two different training routes. There's a full-time church-based route and that tends to be people more from the evangelical wing and then there's the evening and weekend training route for people who are in work or can't otherwise train full-time, and that tends to be from across a broader spectrum of church backgrounds. But they meet for residential weekends and residential weeks together and we do the whole spectrum of worship styles within the Church of England. They learn to trust each other and to see why somebody would worship differently from you and that God might actually enjoy different styles. And you learn to listen to each other's theological points of view, because there are students who disagree about the things that Anglicans disagree about. They're unlikely to ever change each other's minds but they're going to learn a much better way of having conversations about things like women bishops than we do now. We have students on all sides of that debate and the Church of England recognises both as valid Christian points of view, so the training colleges do too. But we do encourage people not just to parade ideas that they haven't really thought through but to really listen to the arguments on both sides.

'For most women they've been through the struggle by the time they get to us but quite a lot of them have grown up in churches where the biblical teaching is very much that women cannot be called to leadership. As they began to feel and hear God's call to leadership they had a real struggle about whether they were deceiving themselves or whether it was actually a call to something else. And a lot of them have spoken very movingly about how difficult it was that a community that had really nurtured them and helped them to grow up as Christians was then saying to them, "But no, you're wrong about this." A lot of those women have had to go through a real testing but I think they've overcome it by just being patient, really testing the call and then having it recognised by a few key people and being encouraged to test it further. And the Church of England does test people's call quite thoroughly, so if the Church of England says, "Yes, we think you are called to the ministry", you do feel reasonably confident that you are. And some people have very moving testimonies of how, by walking with these women through this process, they have become convinced about women in the Church.

'In terms of my teaching I bring a lot of my life experience with me because the privilege of things I've seen over the last ten years seems to be something I can share. One of the drawbacks of being married to the Archbishop of Canterbury is that I couldn't have a voice in big Church debates because people can't distinguish between me and my husband. It was very annoying but I had to accept it as it would make his life more difficult, but I could talk about it with students privately. Perhaps stupidly I have never seen myself as a female role model, but I realise for some people it is quite liberating just to see a woman teaching. I always find it faintly annoying when people come up and say, "It's so wonderful to see a woman doing that," because what I want to know is whether I said anything that was worth anything rather than whether I was just noticed because I was a woman.

'When Rowan became Archbishop of Canterbury it was very different for me and there was an inevitable expectation of things that I would do. There were amazing opportunities that we were offered. I didn't go everywhere with Rowan, partly because of the children and partly because of the job, and partly because we've just never done it like that. I have always needed to work as well and have colleagues of my own and people who know me as me, not just as "wife of", and because the children were quite small I wouldn't have been able to go everywhere with Rowan anyway. Our son was six and our daughter was 14 when we moved to Canterbury, so I was always going to have to be home-based. But I did have the opportunity to go with Rowan to some really interesting and challenging places in the world and to see what it's like to be an Anglican Christian in a Muslim state like Pakistan, for example. It was really instructive to be part of a minority, and there are places where it works very amicably in Pakistan and places where it is really not at all pleasant. I think Christian women in Pakistan feel very much the bottom of the heap and are very vulnerable and very identifiable because they're not wearing coverings. There were huge challenges, so it just felt an immense privilege to be able to meet women there. I particularly tried to go with Rowan to places where the societies are quite segregated when I thought I might be able to have conversations that he wouldn't easily be able to have, particularly with women.

'After a trip like that there is a longing to work out what to do with what I've seen, how to share it and how to make it valuable. So one of the things I'm always trying to remind our students at St Mellitus is to go to things like the Anglican Communion website and follow the prayer diary. Every day several provinces are being prayed for and you get a sense of the range of ways in which the Anglican Church operates around the world. The last official trip we did was to Papua New Guinea where the rate of violence against women is startling and does seem to be culturally hugely acceptable and the Church is in some places battling against it very valiantly but in some places, as everywhere, it's just part of its culture. I found that really disturbing. And so many things then follow from that because obviously if you bring children up in that atmosphere of fear, you're damaging the next generation. Where there's no culture of respect for women AIDS tends to spread much more quickly. So many things follow from the improper treatment of women in development terms.'

These comments led me to ask Jane more about the link between the situation for women around the world and the Church's patriarchal image, not helped by the failure to agree on consecrating women bishops. I wondered whether she saw a connection between the two things, as some other interviewees had done. There also seems to be so much more the Church can do to speak into issues of social justice in this country although I know Rowan had tried to challenge people on these issues on numerous occasions. This certainly brought out her more feisty side and I could see that years of watching her husband deal with criticism had taken its toll.

'I partly agree with the problem of the Church's patriarchal image but the other side is that there are quite a lot of women in fairly senior leadership positions in the Church of England. We have been banging our head against the wall on this women bishops issue but I don't think we should blind ourselves to the fact that actually the Church has been really quite a good employer of women at archdeacon level, deanery level, senior incumbent level, and if you look around the business world they may say that everything's equal there but you don't see it. We're not saying that it's equal but actually we are practicing a model of leadership. Clearly the House of Bishops is iconic and to see that big group of men does look strange nowadays but I think that that can distort our perception of how widely women are deployed. But it's obviously very easy just to go for the headline. There was so much public anger around the debate from people who don't go to church and I think a lot of my friends who are ordained had to put up with constantly trying to defend the Church when they didn't feel it was very defensible at that point. I'm not suggesting that we've got it right but I'm just suggesting it is worth looking at the wider picture.

'In term of issues of social justice and the Church, at parish church level I think there's a lot of remarkably good work being done. Organisations like the Mothers' Union, for example, have a striking record for supporting social justice issues in other parts of the world and in Britain. And when people say to me, "Why doesn't the Church speak out?" I always say to them, "Where?" I mean, apart from putting your soapbox down in the middle of Trafalgar Square, where are you supposed to do it? The media choose what they will report from Church leaders and the media are not interested in giving the Church a platform to air its own views, they're only interested in the controversial things. So Church leaders could teach until they were blue in the face and write articles and statements but they wouldn't go anywhere. And, you know, a lot of Church leaders are increasingly using social media as a way of reaching a great many people. But I think publicly in the House of Lords bishops have really stood out and used the opportunities given to them. And I think people are always saying that the Church should give a lead but they really haven't thought through how that would happen and they haven't thought through what would be the point of an archbishop haranguing people from the media about it, because either people agree with him or they don't and either way, unless you can actually have a conversation with them about it, it's not going to get very much further. And mostly, when people say they'd like a lead from the Church they mean they'd like the Church to say what they personally believe, they want the Church to support their point of view.

'I'm very defensive about the Church of England as you can see. There was a lot of criticism that came with Rowan's job and at times it made me absolutely hopping mad and I longed to say, "You have no idea what you're talking about," but most of the time you know it isn't personal and a lot of it comes from people's longing to see the Church of England being what they hope for, so it comes out of good motives and you try to find the good motives and forget the bad bits.'

Although Jane was quite defensive about the criticism of Rowan I felt the issue of woman bishops must have been a complicated one for her. She knows many of the senior women in the Church of England very well and has heard many of the arguments on both sides. It can't be easy keeping friendships when an issue causes such intense feelings but clearly there were times of laughter too. She has clear views on the impact women can have in the Church and the challenge for women who have to balance complex lives.

'I do remember when women were first ordained in the Church of England I wrote an essay about whether or not the women would change or whether they would actually begin to change the Church. When you become a lawyer or a businesswoman or a politician you have to buy into the culture of how it's done and I think it is the same for the Church. I think it would be very unrealistic and puts extra pressure on them if we thought that once we have women bishops the Church will instantly change the way it does business. I don't think it will. I think the first women bishops will be people who can do business like that because that's how we think it needs to be done. One of the things that I think will change is that women are trying to juggle family life and work and people are beginning to have to come to grips with the very unhealthy expectation that the clergy would work all hours.

'In terms of the gifts that women at the higher level of the Church bring, they're just so different, all of them. I think one of the things they bring is that they're used to putting up with how they're treated. The women who are in leadership in the Church of England have all, without exception I would say, had both very supportive colleagues and very unsupportive colleagues in a way that would be quite startling for most men. But I hope that will change. At the moment that is something quite important that they bring because it holds a little bit of a mirror up to us as the Church, about how we can treat each other.

'Quite a lot of the women that I know who are in higher positions in the Church are very strong leaders from the front and that's how they've survived, and I think some women are very much more likely to be collaborative. But it's really quite hard to generalise. I hope that we're training people for more collaborative ministry altogether because increasingly there will be one paid clergy person working with a team of people on whom he or she has to depend, and you can't have that kind of dictating leadership anymore. I do recognise that some women look more confident than they are and I think nearly all the women I know would always slightly hedge around a statement in case somebody else doesn't agree with it. And I think that is partly years of conditioning and how they have been treated and partly a lot of women would tell you that they have been saying something in a meeting and it isn't heard until a man says it too.

'I had a great fear that all of us who had worked together across that debate, those of us who felt called to ordination and those of us who didn't, that we were working together for one thing, and then suddenly women were going to cross the divide and would become clergy and then at dinner parties they would all congregate at the clergy end leaving those of us who weren't clergy at the other end. And that does happen, it really does. There is clerical gossip that clergy of either sex engage in. And in one sense, why not, because that happens in any profession.

'I don't think I've ever not believed in God but I haven't always liked the God that I thought I believed in and in particular over the last ten years, at points where good Christian people have behaved appallingly, I have thought, "Is this really a good idea?" It can be hard to love. And the discipline that I set myself was to find the good thing that people were being passionate about while they were being so horrid to each other. There is nearly always something that people think they're defending, something glorious about their understanding of God that they're trying to defend, even if the means of defence they use are indefensible. And I think that's what I was trying to do through the women bishops debate because as a theologian I do see the evidence on both sides and as a Christian with a very wide set of Christian friends, I have friends, women and men, on both sides.

'I think there is also the perception that ours is a society that thinks equality means uniformity and if we're not saying exactly the same thing about everybody and allowing everybody to do absolutely everything just the same then we're not making people equal. And so you could argue that we are squashing men and women into less than themselves by saying they have to do everything the same. People look at our society as it has developed and they don't see that we have fantastic relationships between men and women, they don't see that the way in which our understanding of how men and women relate has led to flourishing families and flourishing marriages. They look and think, "Well this definition of equality might not be the best thing," and it is quite difficult to say that positively to women who are experiencing God's call into leadership. But standing back, it is a question worth asking. Is there a way of saying that men and women are interdependent? I don't like the complementarity argument because it's a way of stereotyping what each will do, but it seems to me that the whole body of Christ imagery suggests that we are absolutely interdependent and it's no good all of us trying to be a hand or a head because then the thing doesn't function. It's not an argument, it's an experience that both women and men have voiced, that we are really not exploring the full range of gifts on offer by simply assuming that only one kind of leadership is right.

'If the Bible is really one of the things that God gives us to stop us going away and making up our own religion then we are bound to take it seriously and it isn't completely clear on this topic. So there has to be a provisionality about the decision that we make until we can make it with a greater proportion of the worldwide Church agreeing that this is how scripture is read, which is where unity comes in. I think that what Paul writes about the relationships between men and women was revolutionary in his day, that mutuality that he was talking about would've been mindboggling. But he certainly does see a level of hierarchy there. And so, although I am personally a 100 per cent sure that God is calling women into leadership in the Church, that has to be personal until it is possible to see clearly how the wider Christian community reads the scripture. I think that the people who are still in the Church of England now have accepted that there will be women bishops so what they're looking for is a way of expressing what I've just said, which is that there has to be a provisionality about this decision.

'It seems to me you can't say that all Christians must believe this because there is an uncertainty. With women priests they've allowed for what they call the "two integrities". The parishes have a right not to have a woman, that's enshrined in law. So it's just how you take that into the next level when you're talking about bishops where it does become much more complicated. A bishop has oversight of all of those churches and what it means for a bishop to be a bishop and yet not have that pastoral oversight in a particular church is what we couldn't work out. I'm quite glad to be out of the decision-making, although I am obviously not out of it as someone who's training people for ordination in the Church.'

Although teaching is a big part of Jane's life, she has also published a number of books over the years, including *Approaching Christmas* and one of her most loved books *Angels*. This is a subject that has always appealed to me, whether I am thinking about a beautiful girl I knew who died at the age of two and has always felt like my guardian angel or the appeal of angels in art. The Bible has a lot to say about angels, including coming to the aid of people, announcing Jesus' birth and helping build up the early Church. There is a wonderful saying in Hebrews 13.2: 'Do not neglect to show hospitality to strangers, for by doing that some have entertained angels without knowing it', which seems a great lesson for how we should treat people. Jane explained her interest in the subject.

'I think every Christian is a theologian. Anybody who's saying anything about God is making an assumption about the nature and purpose of God in what you pray, in what you say, and therefore I'm really quite passionate about encouraging people to feel confident about what they say about God. And when it came to my book about angels in the Bible I discovered that Christians and non-Christians could get excited talking about angels across all kinds of different divides and faiths. And so I thought it was interesting to help people think, what is it about angels that you find attractive? And it does seem to be that sense of a presence in the universe that is benevolent and that taps into such a huge longing for a sense of being cared for. And I've had so many touching letters from people describing their experiences of angels and they are all of that kind of nature. I find it very moving.

'Individual experiences can be very powerful. Interestingly the Alpha Course is primarily an academic course which enables you to ask questions and look at evidence, but built into it is a weekend where you're encouraged to experience the presence of the Holy Spirit. And it is that that often makes the difference because it is actually an encounter with God that you can't deny because it has happened to you, although I think you need to make it clear from the beginning that God doesn't force himself on people and it won't happen until you really want it to. I think that's a quite important thing to say given how many people think God is violent and intrusive and forces himself upon people when that is not a true Christian experience of him. As a theologian I would want to say that you can never prove the existence of God in simple logical terms because God doesn't want to be proved like that, but God does come to meet people and they know when they've been met and it's really interesting to see that as a key part of one of the most successful evangelistic tools of the last few decades.

'In the book [*Angels*] I wrote that we don't need to believe that our loved ones become angels. Christian theology says that we are right to be afraid of death, that the death that separates us from people that we love is not how God intended it to be, but Christian theology also says that God himself makes that decision to go down into death so that even in death we are not separated from the love of God. That's where my total confidence in life beyond death comes from. God does not forget people, they are in God, so it is my doctrine of God and what I see in the New Testament of the death and resurrection of Jesus that makes me confident about that, while, like any other human being, I fear it as a human experience of ending. It is a step of faith to say, "I will trust God with those that I love".'

Favourite verse: Romans 8.38–9 'For I am convinced that neither death, nor life … nor anything else in all creation, will be able to separate us from the love of God in Christ Jesus our Lord.'

Favourite woman: I am afraid I have to say my favourite Biblical figure is a man and I don't have a favourite woman. I just think Paul is one of the great maligned and misunderstood figures in the Bible but I think he's such a complex and interesting person and responsible for so much of how we see theology. You can see him really wrestling, you can see bits where the sentence goes on for half a page because he's got himself completely tied up in the argument. He's never going to let it just drift and I just love that complete passion and the fact that he changed his life completely. He is an intellectual person who's going to do such rigorous theology but it was the encounter with Jesus that took him there.

8

The Reverend Professor Sarah Coakley

Sarah Coakley is a highly respected academic theologian, philosopher of religion and ordained priest who has worked both at Harvard and at Cambridge University where she was the first woman appointed to the Chair of Norris-Hulse Professor of Divinity in 2007. Sarah is particularly known for her interest in feminist theology and is currently working on a four-volume systematic theology (an overview of the main doctrines of Christian faith). I had read some of her work and became rather nervous about our meeting, as I struggled with some of the complex arguments around issues such as God, sexuality and the self. However, I admired the clear and logical way she spoke to the House of Bishops before the debate on women bishops and was keen to know more about her own experience as a woman in this field. I was also intrigued by her decision to be ordained alongside her academic career.

When I met her in the modern School of Divinity building at Cambridge she was very warm and friendly and not at all intimidating. Her office had large glass windows overlooking a charming walled garden and comfortable furniture that made it seem surprisingly cosy. She clearly has a very busy life and had just returned from baptising her grandson in Washington, DC after leading a series of meditations on Holy Week at Salisbury Cathedral. She and her American husband now live in Ely where she was appointed an honorary canon of the cathedral and she commutes to Cambridge to teach and write. I asked her how her passion for academia had developed and particularly her interest in feminist theology.

'My family was Anglican. My mother was quietly very devout but I think my father worshipped more on the golf course. I had three brothers and we were brought up serving at the altar or singing in church choirs. There was a lot of theological discussion between me and my brothers and in fact my eldest brother and I started a theological discussion group at our church, All Saints Blackheath, when we were 16 and 14 respectively. I remember thinking that I wanted to be a theologian when I was about 12, at about the time I was confirmed. I know this sounds absurd and it's very annoying to my offspring, who have had difficulty finding out what their vocations are, but I've had a tremendous vocational propulsion all my life. The only difference was that it wasn't until I was about 21 that I began to see that this might even be possible. I didn't have a sense of calling to the priesthood and it never occurred to me at that time anyway. The issue was being discussed but I was in an Anglo-Catholic wing of the Church and I was very pained by the fact that I wasn't allowed to be an acolyte but I didn't fight it. I was allowed to be in the choir and I think that had a very formative side to it; learning to inhabit the psalms, for instance, is tremendously spiritually enriching.

'But there was something about a call to God that I immediately thought of in terms of intellectual exploration, although I didn't really have any reason to think that I could pursue it. I only read the few theological books that were available in our house and there weren't many. The two that were particularly memorable at this early stage were ones that my mother had, including *The Letters of Evelyn Underhill*. Underhill was a woman spiritual director of great intellectual stature but someone who obviously could not, at the time, be an academic theologian but she certainly had lots of interactions with academic theologians and she was a kind of role model for me. And then the other book that fell into my lap was *Honest to God* by John Robinson, which came out when I was 12 and I read it very immaturely at that age and thought, "This is wonderful, here is a bishop inviting lay people to think." And that wasn't an experience one normally had as a lay person, or even now has as a lay person in many churches.

'So although I did classics and music at school in the sixth form, I always knew I wanted to study theology. It wasn't encouraged very much at school as I think it was thought to be something you ought to do vocationally later but I did get into New Hall, Cambridge which I found an absolutely wonderful, nurturing place. I was the only woman in my year doing theology and there were, I think, in the first year of the Tripos [degree] only six women and a few more later. It was a relatively small group of people and most of the men were en route to being ordained. It was a heavily clerical faculty and, to be perfectly frank, I found much of the Tripos teaching dull. I was longing to do more creative, systematic work. The Tripos was still almost entirely Biblically based but I thought I might as well do what they do really well here. I already had Greek from school and I took up Hebrew and did that intensively for the three years I was at Cambridge.

'Then I went to Harvard on a scholarship and it was a refreshingly different world. My interest in feminist theology really developed significantly there. It was an exciting time. I arrived just at the time that [the radical feminist academic] Mary Daly stormed out of Harvard Memorial Church having preached against patriarchal religion and invited the whole congregation to leave. This was a major moment. I wasn't there on that occasion but she published *Beyond God, the Father*, in my first year at Harvard, so this was an exciting time. To begin with my thoughts about those arguments were somewhat critical but it was impossible to ignore what was going on. And I think that my real personal commitment to feminism came painfully in a rather different way a little bit later, round about the time I was finishing my doctoral thesis.

'After Harvard I came back to England, got married and my husband and I got a job at the University of Lancaster. And it was while I was finishing my thesis and having our first child that I got drawn into practices of silent prayer, which changed everything for me. One of the things that happens when you are praying silently is that there's a kind of sorting house of all your desires being operated upon, and you can't keep up a polite edifice. And I became very interested in a problematic that it seemed to me was deeply implicated in feminist questions in the Church, which no one was really talking about. And this was a problematic about how desire for God and sexual desire are related, or should be related. And anyone who spends any time on their knees will know that this is a nexus of huge significance.

'It's not only sexual desire that is at stake; it's also desire for power or influence or money, all these somewhat ambiguous powers within us are in negotiation and the big question is, "Do I long for God above everything else and, if I do, how are these other potentially idolatrous goods to be negotiated?" Not that they should be suppressed or destroyed but how are they related? And I began to read the Fathers, the ancient patristic authors, with a new eye. I think when I was at Cambridge originally I tended to think of that period as uninteresting and superseded by modern critical rational thinking. But I began to see that that nexus of associations was being explored by some of the great early patristic authors because they were "kneeling theologians". And that it was in the modern period where devotion became disarticulated from rational and systematic and philosophical thinking, which was a great loss. It's the same moment at which you lose the integration of pastoral theology and high academic theology which is a problematic we are still struggling with. I think that's very difficult for women as women tend to have a stronger desire to integrate pieces of themselves.

'And so out of a kind of personal crisis about the challenges and pain of silent prayer – because it's an immensely purgative, profound, painful process – I began to think that the real problem for feminist theology, which should perhaps be distinguished from feminism and egalitarianism, is how exactly am I to overcome patriarchal idolatry and how is that to be connected up with the issue that patriarchal male thinking has often created woman in a model of its own making, which is a lot to do with a failure to integrate sexual desire and desire for God? So woman represents a fearful challenge, not simply as someone who might be cleverer than you, although that's pretty frightening, but because she is also attractive.

'As the former Bishop of London Graham Leonard, who converted to Rome, once said, "I wouldn't know what to do if a woman was at the altar; I would feel I needed to embrace her." Now that tells you a lot about that nexus. So after I'd finished my thesis I started to work in this area and to look at an integration of what in the modern period has been called spirituality and systematic theology and to do a lot of probing in the patristic and medieval world for materials that might illuminate this nexus. I began to see the fight for women's ordination in this much more complex landscape, not just that women ought to be allowed to do everything that men do but why is this such a problem? And I began to see that erotic projection and negative erotic deflation was a huge part of it, and I thought I was on to something that not everybody else was on to.

'My husband and I spent 15 years at Lancaster where we conducted a sustained social experiment of job-sharing, which meant we were very poor. I think our first-year salary at Lancaster was £3,000 between us and we lived in a very deprived end of town, which was itself an extremely interesting undertaking. But we had both our children there and we were able to avoid having a nanny because one of us was always at home, which was lovely for them. But at the end of that 15 years I was invited to go to Oriel College, Oxford, and we had a rather difficult two years when my husband was commuting back to Lancaster and I wasn't at all happy. I was the first female teaching officer at Oriel and it was rather like limping around under the weight of very peculiar projections.

'I think any woman who's been the first woman on a board or the chapter of a cathedral or a senior common room or something will know this phenomenon. It's extremely hard to manage. I wasn't harassed sexually but I was treated in some extremely weird ways which were actually very undermining to my position and I had to fight to be allowed to do the job that I'd been appointed to do. And at some point it was very helpful that I had lawyers in my family. I kept my powder dry but I made it clear that I knew exactly how they had abrogated employment law and I was very relieved to get out after two years having been offered a Chair at Harvard. By the time I left Oriel everything was going very well indeed but I had to have all these fights to be accepted to do what I had come to do. Fortunately for me my students flourished so they couldn't say that I couldn't do the job; and in retrospect it was quite a creative time for my writing as well.

'So then we de-camped to America and Harvard did a wonderful thing for us by creating a job for my husband too. My story is so much bound up with my amazing husband who has been willing to share things with me and go along with my career, in ways that haven't always been comfortable for him or ostensibly to his best advantage.

'At Harvard I met extremely vibrant and well-established forms of feminism because Harvard Divinity School has probably been the most significant place for feminist theoretical discussion in relation to religion. I was not initially very popular on that front because I did not subscribe to some of the shibboleths of American feminism. Although I'm not an unadulterated fan of the French feminists, their major critique is against a kind of egalitarian American feminism which assumes that woman should be more like a man. It puts great stress on equality and is rather uninterested in the facts of childbirth, lactation, maternity, all these features. So the paradox of equality and difference is the ongoing debate. Actually, as I arrived at Harvard, even that debate was becoming tired and it was being replaced by the new interest in post-modern gender theory, as it was now going to be called, and no longer egalitarian feminism. It was an exciting time to be in the midst of that and I think I created a particular voice, which had come out of my own prayer experience and is still very controversial in America. It is summed up in the book I wrote called *Powers and Submissions*, in which I argue that submission to God is itself the fundamentally empowering fact of human life and that this submission is different from all the other submissions. The link there is that a lot of egalitarian American feminism was extremely suspicious of all forms of authority and suspicious of a transcendent notion of God to whom one gives submission. But as post-modern interests in gender and practice became vogue my position appeared less offensive and perhaps a little more intriguing.'

Sarah's academic career had clearly gone from strength to strength and she had a busy enough life raising a family, teaching and writing. It seemed surprising that she would complicate her life even more by considering ordination but I assumed she had felt called to go in this direction. The combination of her academic background and her role as a priest should have given her contribution to the debate on women bishops some extra weight although I imagined it probably had the reverse effect. She described her route to ordination.

'When I left Oxford to go to Harvard I had been very much involved in the movement for the ordination of women as priests. I'd done big public events for it. I left in 1993 so it had just gone through, much to everyone's surprise. I was a lay feminist woman theologian, strongly supporting the ordination of women but having no intention whatsoever of becoming one myself. Oxford was full of clerics running around like black beetles and I thought, "Well you don't need clergical theologians here; what you need is women's voices that are unencumbered by being subject to episcopal authority so that they can speak the truth."

'But then I arrived at Harvard Divinity School and found a new generation of young people coming in to train for ordination, many of them gay or lesbian, all of them highly idealistic and spiritually attuned and very smart, with high grades. All of them were longing for some role model or manifestation of the integration of prayer and the highest intellectual endeavours. And they looked around and they could see professors having those highest intellectual endeavours but having lost their faith. At the time the vast majority of professors at Harvard Divinity School, even if they'd been ordained earlier in their lives, had drifted away from the Church or actually renounced the Church and so I found myself in this really strange spot. Even in the first week that I arrived there were queues of people just wanting to come and talk about how they should pull all these pieces together. It was very exciting and wonderful and very early on in that first year a gay man came and said, "Will you please come and pray with us? We need someone from the faculty to pray with the students." And I thought, "I need to think about this." And then I said, "You know, at Harvard Divinity School we're so diverse, if we have a prayer group in which we talk we're going to have an argument so why don't we have a silent prayer group?" And the silent prayer group started and it had a life of its own which was just incredible.

'About five years after I'd arrived, there were so many people asking me about being ordained and it was almost like

I was being given this gift by others. It became more uncomfortable to resist this than to go on as I was, and so I had to
take the great risk of deciding, "Do I put myself forward and
perhaps gets turned down?" and there's no way round that
horror. And I also had to decide which country to do this in
and which Church, because by this time I had realised how
very different Episcopalianism and English Anglicanism are in
all kinds of ways.

'We were still living in Oxford every summer so we were
peripatetic. I put out some feelers in the Episcopal Church but
it was a bad moment then and I knew it could take years longer
than in England. I just wanted to know whether the Church
even wanted me and so I went to Richard Harries, the Bishop
of Oxford, who was absolutely wonderful and really wanted me
to try out this vocation. And it all happened very fast. I was sent
to a selection conference, always a frightening prospect, within
less than a year. It was quite funny that the first question in the
first interview at the selection conference, which was conducted
by a Chaplain to the Queen, was "Now, why do you think you
want to be a priest when you ought to be at home looking after
your children?" So I sat there and I thought of about 16 cutting
remarks that I could make and I didn't say any of them. There
was a long silence and then I said, "Well one of my children is
already at university and the other one is 16." I thought, "This
man is clearly winding me up." And he was, as apparently he
afterwards wrote me a good report. And I thought, "Are you
doing this to the men? No, I'm sure you're not." But I meet this
all the time. There's still much clerical resistance to women and
there's often a clerical resistance to anyone who's an academic.
So you've got a double whammy.

'It still goes on in all kinds of different ways. They are very
hard to chart and it's difficult to know whether it's because you
have a certain personality that tends to rub people up the wrong
way but why should you blame yourself? It's usually what I call
unconscious "dirty tricks", so it's, "Oops I must have lost an
email from you." Or, "Didn't I tell you that you were meant to
bring a cope?" The issues are ostensibly minor but underlying
them is a defensiveness.

'So I was ordained in England but the arrangement was that

in the months in the summer when I was in England I would technically be serving my title at the parish of Littlemore which was just outside Oxford, a very difficult parish as it has a very large mental hospital to visit regularly. And then the arrangement was that during the school year I would be an Associate, as it's called in America, in a very different kind of parish not far from where we lived, which was in a leafy suburb with very intellectual, mostly rather well-off, people where I did a lot of teaching. And so the combination of these extremely different parishes was enormously rich.

'I had another piece of incredible bounty. I had been doing quite a lot of work for the Lily Foundation. They give a lot of money to theological education and I'd been involved in a couple of collaborative book-writing projects with them. One of their major concerns at the time was that there weren't enough senior professors in the university divinity schools in America who'd got their hands dirty with actual pastoral work. They were concerned about this disjoint between so-called pastoral theology and academic or systematic theology or philosophy of religion. And so when they heard I was getting ordained they said, "We've got this money left in a pot at the end of a project about practices that we'd like to dole out. Why don't you apply for it and you can take a year out from teaching and go through all the things that your students go through." This was an absolute gift, it was just fantastic.

'And so I concocted what I think was a rather over-demanding year in which I was doing something called CPE [Clinical Pastoral Education], which I think anyone who's been through it would say they wouldn't have missed but it's also very painful and difficult. You are in a hospital setting and you are on the wards with people in extremis and then, as you are experiencing learning how to be a Chaplain to such people, you are also every week going through a kind of internal processing of that with the other people doing it. But the most important thing about it is actually being with the patients who are dying or for whom terrible things have happened. And in my case I was on an atypical psychotic Alzheimer's ward: my placement there was probably designed to humiliate the Harvard professor! But I was very glad that I did do that, although it was terrifying and there was a lot of violent behaviour going on towards the patients which I eventually reported. In the second half of the year I also spent a day a week in a jail in Boston.

'I think this was far more intensive an experience than most Anglican ordinands get and it really changed my life, it really turned me inside out. I'm still writing about it because in my systematic theology that I'm writing now these pieces are all actually being integrated into a whole vision. So finally I'm able to do what I always wanted to do, which is to ensure that there is an integration in systematic theology between the spiritual, the intellectual, the philosophical, the sociological and the pastoral, and I've concocted a method for pulling all these together.'

As a well-respected theologian it was not surprising that Sarah had been asked to make a key speech to the House of Bishops as part of the debate in 2012. Many women were very concerned at a proposal to have two categories of bishop so certain parishes could have alternative episcopal oversight from a male bishop, clearly undermining the authority of the proposed women bishops. She made three key points partly in response to this suggestion and to reflect on the general issue of expectations that had followed the ordination of women priests. I asked her to explain her arguments.

'I think the first point is so obvious that one really despairs of anyone ever resisting it, which is that by definition what a bishop is is the locus of unity in the Church. And if you mess about with that idea then you're probably better not to have bishops at all because the whole point of a bishop when there is a dispute, or when there is trouble or when there is a problem of authority, is that it passes up to him or her. If you're not going to do that, you're going to have two hierarchies that are simply in mutual enmity and you might as well not have had a hierarchy at all. So the idea that we can have some women bishops who are contained and constrained is a contradiction in terms. I tried to illustrate that from some of the earliest theology of bishops. Now the funny thing is that when I made that first point at the House of Bishops, it was the Anglo-Catholics who were nodding their heads. They were so relieved to hear someone talking theological sense rather than practical compromises; but of course they probably also hoped that my line of approach would stall the whole process. So my view is that we've got to keep our head on this issue at this point and I think we may feel at the end of the day that the awful thing we went through, where it got stopped, was possibly providential because I think there must be an acceptance of women bishops on an absolutely equal par with men bishops.

'The second point was a different way of saying the same thing but from another direction, which is that we have a very honourable tradition of ecclesiology within Anglicanism which we all seem to be having amnesia about at the moment and I think if we could get over it we'd actually see a way through. A lot of our troubles in the Anglican Communion recently over the gay issue, over the so-called covenant which is related to that, have been either trying to emulate Rome in their system of authority or becoming entangled with Calvinist views about covenant, which were never really what Anglicanism opted for. A purist form of Anglicanism went that way and Presbyterianism within England went that way, but it was Richard Hooker who wrote, right at the end of the sixteenth century, his Ecclesiastical Polity, which became the hallmark for how to think about the Church in the Anglican tradition. The key is that the primacy of authority is given in scripture but the place of reason in Anglicanism is also very high, such that tradition is seen as mediated by "reasonable saints" in every generation. So for Hooker the three loci of authority are scripture, reason and tradition. And, for him, natural law and reason are themselves developmental. So we live in a dynamic church which confronts new problems in different generations: its life involves a truth which is unfolding.

'So this idea that reason has a very high place in its conversation with scripture should mean that Anglicanism resists fundamentalism: certainly Hooker himself did. Why is this important for now? Well, if you come up with a vision of two different kinds of bishop which have mutually incompatible and logically incompatible statuses, that is not rational. We need to take very seriously the place of reason in relation to scripture in our Church and that's a very distinctive feature of Anglican ecclesiology to which we need to be recalled. Over the last 20 years our Church in England has allowed women to be ordained priests but under certain restrictions and without the intrinsic capacity to be chosen as bishops. This has made a nonsense of the traditional understanding of the clerical calling, and it is not sustainable.

'The third point I made was a general one about bureaucratisation versus genuine theological thinking. The discussions at Synod about women clerics had increasingly become debates about bureaucratic lacunae or ways of fudging arrangements rather than thinking theologically. In addition, the last decades have seen an almost unconscious slide towards managerialism in the Church, to turning the ministry into a job rather than a vocation. And I think women are suffering particularly badly from this because the authentic Anglican way of being a priest is to be with your people, which women tend to be very good at, and not to be tied up in endless red tape and bureaucratic emails and box-ticking. And I think that our Church has become subject to this just as the NHS [National Health Service] has become subject to it and the other areas of life that are patrolled by government.

'I actually ended up saying that the Church was in danger of signing its own theological death warrant if it voted against women bishops. I felt it wasn't insignificant that during the period running up to the vote, Rowan [Williams] had decided for a long patch not to have a doctrine commission because it was too expensive. And what eventually replaced it was too large and unwieldy to be effective.

'Rowan is one of my oldest friends and I deeply revere him. I don't want to say anything insulting to him at all and I understand the incredibly difficult situation he found himself in. But you should notice a point at which he said something in the course of the women bishops debate which I would challenge him on and he would be happy to have me challenge him on. He said, "We have to keep our theology vigorous and independent and not simply at the mercy of whatever fashion or currents in society to which we are vulnerable." Now the problem is that we weren't keeping our theology vigorous in an Anglican way. The notion of the dynamic nature of rational tradition is why I'm an Anglican, and that is not the same thing as merely following passing fashions. Instead, the whole integrity of the theology of the episcopate is at stake.

'If we look at the history of the Church it's an extremely patchy story in relation to the role of women in which I think that tension of radical breakthrough and closing down has had waves, depending on the gender theory that was regnant, frankly, in the Church or the world at the time. There's no doubt that there was a kind of elbowing towards patriarchy and I would say that the New Testament is a manifestation of a huge crisis between the more radical remarks of Jesus and Paul about women and an immediate attempt to close that down. There have then been short periods in the Church which for really interesting ecclesiastical, social, political reasons have allowed women to have a greater play of authority, such as Hildegard of Bingen in the twelfth century, but then not long after her the "episcopal" authority of abbesses is revoked and although there are influential women saints they don't have the institutional power that she did. So the twentieth century is an enormous moment of breakthrough, especially for Protestant women.

'In 2005 I started, with Sam Wells, a movement in the Church called the Littlemore Group. Our vision is that we need scholar priests, women and men together, committing themselves back to difficult parishes and doing rich theological thinking on the spot in the parishes and supporting one another there. This is part of my desire that we don't create more fragmentation in the Church and a theological neglect of the parish. When you're chosen for ordination there's now a box that's ticked saying, "Are you a future theological educator?" If you're potentially that then the Church is willing to spend more money on your training. Then they expect you to be in some kind of fast lane, so you might be an Oxford or Cambridge chaplain and then you might end up in the cathedral and, who knows, you might be a dean or a bishop. But I think that this initial divergence between "theological educators" and the rest is very pernicious, partly because almost all of the women and men who are trained over a certain age never get that box ticked and get less good training. And that contributes to a rump of not very well theologically educated older women, which doesn't help the women's cause. But I also think the other unfortunate side of it is that we are fast-tracking into positions of authority people who don't necessarily have the humbling and creative experience of commitment to the parish.

'A kind of CEO-thinking has infected the Church so badly that we now think, "We haven't got much money so let's just let our less theologically educated clergy do all that nasty work." And that's why so many women have been given almost impossible jobs. Men are as well, to be sure, but women, in particular, are sent out to look after up to ten parishes. When I ask these women at diocesan conferences how they are getting on they look round to see who might be listening and then they say, "I'm just about coping." We can't blame anybody for this because it's actually a financial crisis in the Church which has caused it and underlying it is the result of the loss of belief in the country. But I think its playing out in some rather weird ways in relationship to the women/men priest roles and I'm not sure how many people have woken up to this or actually done the head-counting.

'When I came back to this country from America and the first few times I appeared in a cassock, mostly because people asked me to preach for evensong here in colleges, it was a completely different feeling from when I stand up in my cassock in an American church and preach. I often feel a negative projection coming towards me, something like: "Oh here comes another woman priest, I bet she's stupid, we don't want to listen to her." And I don't feel that at all when I'm in America, even when I'm in an Anglo-Catholic church which is quite likely not wanting to hear what I have to say for other reasons. So I think the image of a woman priest is not in good shape at the moment in this country, even though the secular-world and most of the Church wants to go forward with women bishops. I think we have kind of internalised this second-rate feeling in some way. We've now become a scandal in the eyes of the world as well as the eyes of the Church. And I think what people don't talk about very much is that we've had 20 years of women priests being treated as second-rate, intrinsically unable to be bishops and as such they are already demoted. And I think that's deeply significant and I feel it very strongly. It can of course change, but in order for it to change, the symbolic import of the presence of a significant number of outstanding women bishops will be vital.'

Favourite verse: *Romans 8.26 '... for we do not know how to pray as we ought, but that very Spirit intercedes ...' That's what silent prayer is. If we try and do it, it's a jumble but if we allow space to hear and for the spirit to operate in us, everything changes.*

Favourite woman: *Mary of Bethany. She chooses the 'one thing necessary'. She is also the woman who almost certainly – as in John's gospel – washed Christ's feet [not Mary Magdalene] and therefore ecstatically shows her love for him and he approves it.*

9

Dr Alison Elliot, OBE

Alison Elliot was the first female Moderator of the General Assembly in the history of the Church of Scotland and was unusual in being an elder rather than an ordained minister. Appointed for the usual one-year term in 2004, it was an exciting moment for women in the Church and a step ahead of the Church of England who were still arguing about appointing women bishops.

Although she was perceived to be the most senior figure in the Church of Scotland, the role is not the same as the Archbishop of Canterbury and the Church of Scotland is not part of the Anglican Communion. The Church as we know it now began with the Scottish Reformation and the first General Assembly in 1560, which is the highest court of the Church. The Presbyterian system means that no one person or group within the Church should have more influence than the other and there is officially no head as that role is for God. The structure is outwardly more democratic, with individual Churches run by Kirk sessions made up of ordained elders of the Church and presided over by a minister. These meetings can be effective but more often than not are hard to manage as people remain on the session for much of their lives. As an elder myself I had witnessed the serious problems that occur and was keen to get Alison's perspective on the situation.

The moderator's main role is to chair the General Assembly, held once a year in May, but it is not to speak out on issues of faith or ethics as the Scottish Roman Catholic Cardinal often does in Scotland. The moderator role is more ambassadorial and does not really allow for the setting of a strategic vision for the Church and personal views are rarely known. This seemed to me to be a potential strength but also a significant weakness at a time of increasing challenge for the Church in a secular society.

Alison Elliot was not only the first female moderator but she was also the first elder to be appointed to the role since the sixteenth century. She was ordained to the lay role of elder at Greyfriars Church in Edinburgh in 1983 but she is not an ordained minister. Her background was in academia before she became closely involved in significant church committees and eventually became Convenor (Chair) of the Scottish Council of Voluntary Organisations and a fellow of New College, Edinburgh, as well as chairing several other bodies. She has four honorary degrees and is a Fellow of the Royal Society of Edinburgh and an honorary fellow of New College, Edinburgh, as well as Assistant Director of the Centre for Theology and Public Issues at the University. She is married with two children. I asked her more about her background and her religious influences when I met her at her home in Edinburgh.

'My father was a psychiatrist and he was a chief superintendent at Bangour Village Hospital near Edinburgh, so we were brought up in the hospital. It was a very unusual background but an interesting one because you were in the company of people who had mental illness and I'm sure that shaped some of my attitudes. I did a degree in mathematics at Edinburgh University, which included some work on general linguistics, so I became interested in language issues. There was a moment in my third year at university when I had this real revelation because I was sitting doing a tutorial question and the question was, "Is this set open or closed?" And I asked the question no mathematician should ever ask which was, "Who cares?" It didn't have any connection with the reality around us and that was the start of the development of a social conscience for me and it was tied in with the fact that when I wasn't doing mathematics most of my social life at university was tied up with the student Christian movement.

'So I then went to Sussex University and did a degree in experimental psychology before coming back to Edinburgh to do my PhD in children's language development. After that I lectured for two-and-a-half years at Lancaster University before finally returning to Edinburgh as a lecturer but I left that role in 1985 after my daughter was born. I had loved my area of psychology.

We had both our feet in the European tradition which was very philosophical and reflective but we also had our feet in the Anglo-Saxon and American tradition of empirical work and so we were mixing the two, which was very satisfying. We had a research nursery in the department and I was associated with that for about 20 years, first of all from doing my PhD with children in the nursery and then going on to be the academic in charge and eventually being the mother of children there.

'I did have a religious upbringing. My mother had a Free Church of Scotland background [a Presbyterian and Reformed domination], which meant Sundays were different from most people. You could read books on Sundays but only if they were non-fiction. As we got older we managed to go to bed early and do our homework under the covers but actually I learnt to love Sundays and to see them as special time out but it was a fairly strict religious upbringing for the 1950s.

'I got involved in the student Christian movement at university, which was very interested in service and in politics. I was an undergraduate between 1966 and 1970 and that was the time when the ordination of women was happening in the Church of Scotland, but I have to say that it passed me by completely. It's not because I wasn't involved in Church things, but I was involved in a sort of political and social gospel rather than worrying about ordination in the Church. My faith is one that is very much based on service rather than any wish to have a priestly role, so I've never wanted to be an ordained minister. When it comes to my work I tend to take on projects and jobs because other people think I can do it because most of them are fairly daunting prospects. I rely on other people's judgement of whether I can manage or not, but I've never felt that about being ordained. I've always felt that to be ordained as a minister was something which had to be a calling. It had to be something that was not mediated by other people saying that would be OK and that simply never happened to me.

'I think the service part of my life is just the sort of person that I am and I think it has something to do with my interest in mathematics. I think of myself as being a very rational person and even now I don't often appreciate a lot of the approaches to religion which make it a very spiritual experience. I think I have a very strong spiritual sense, but it's one which is embedded in people and in relationships. I see the spirituality as being something that's inherent to life and is normal. It's not something which you isolate out of it and in that sense I've never been particularly drawn to the "mystery" as something which you examine, although there is mystery in everything. I think it's also characteristic of the Church of Scotland. We don't really do spirituality the way that various other traditions do, although there are some that do and the evangelical side is growing again.

'The Church of Scotland has had a history of a very close involvement with the national life of the country and so getting involved, as I did later on, with something like the Church and Nation Committee of the Church of Scotland is putting you right in that nexus between politics and religion. That strand in the Church of Scotland is a very strong one for various historical reasons and the dominant Church of Scotland culture that was around while I was growing up was one which was more liberal and more engaged with the society around it.

'As a student I was involved with the student Christian movement and when I graduated and then got involved in my university career, I would attend Church regularly and sing in the Church choir. One of the people who was very important to me was Duncan Forrester, the chaplain at Sussex University when I was there. He was a Church of Scotland minister and I was a Scottish student so we got to know each other fairly quickly. Later on, when I had my daughter and left my university job, he saw me as someone who had time on her hands and he got me involved in the Centre for Theology and Public Issues that he was setting up at Edinburgh University. It was trying to engage theology with the political world and he saw me as somebody who didn't have the theological background but I had a social sciences background and the Christian commitment. Through that I was appointed to the Church and Nation Committee of the Church of Scotland, which had been founded in 1919 and was very much focused on the Church's commitment to society rather than the Church's role or status in society. It was about what the Church can do to help society become a healthier place. I joined in 1988 and at the same time I was also asked to represent the Church of Scotland as part of the team at the European Ecumenical Assembly in Basel, so right from the start the ecumenical side of my work and the Church and society work were going hand in hand.

'On the ecumenical side of things I was a very useful person because the ecumenical movement is very committed to quotas of women on its governing bodies and to a quota of lay people so the fact that I was not a minister was useful. So I was put on the central committee of the Conference of European Churches for 12 years and I ended up moderating their General Assembly in 2009. I also chaired ACTS which was the Action of Churches Together in Scotland. Within the Church and Nation Committee I started out as the convener of the international interests side of it. It was a wonderful committee because it was voluntary and people were coming in with all kinds of backgrounds and different experiences and we would prepare about a dozen reports each year. For example, I was involved in preparing papers on the ethics of international sanctions during the war in Bosnia and in Kosovo. We were making government aware of the issues and it was a space where people could develop ideas which had a faith base.

'In terms of practical issues the Church and Nation Committee and the Church of Scotland had had a very strong involvement in Malawi and in the Central African Federation and they were instrumental in setting that up way back in 1953. During my time as convener of international relations, Malawi came onto the agenda again. I went there as a monitor of a multi-party election on behalf of the ecumenical movement and was working alongside the UN so my training on that Committee was important.'

It was unusual for the moderator to be a lay person, although not without precedent if you return to the sixteenth century. Approximately 25 per cent of ministers are women and there were female priests in a number of parishes who could have been more obvious choices at the time. I was keen to know how the Church of Scotland had come to appoint Alison in 2004 and whether it was something she had actively sought. She explained that she had been approached before, partly as a result of her experience in previous roles.

'I was convenor of the Church and Nation Committee between 1996 and 2000 and that was when the new Parliament was being introduced in Scotland so it was an opportunity for me to get to know people in the political world and also in civil society because we were all working together for the Parliament. I knew a lot of the MPs in London as well as a lot of the Church leaders. So, although I was a woman elder and therefore apparently somebody who didn't have status in the Church, I knew a lot about the way the Church was operating, both in its political and in its ecumenical spheres. So I was asked in 2000 if I would allow my name to go forward to be the Moderator – you don't apply for this – but I said no as I needed a break and anyway I felt surely they could find a woman minister to do this as there were plenty of them. It just wasn't right.

'But by 2003 I was being asked again and things had moved on. There was a lot of momentum in the press saying, "Look, the Church of Scotland can have women as moderators so why has it never done it?" And in the spring of 2003 Kathy Galloway [an ordained minister and the first woman to lead the Iona Community] got a letter together signed by about 140 women which was saying, "We're all women in the Church, we've all been serving the Church in various ways, why has nobody ever asked us to be moderator?" Now since they had asked me to take the role in the past I couldn't sign that letter and I thought, "There's no point in continuing to say you want to have a woman moderator and then when you're asked you don't pick it up," so when I was asked later on I was more open to the possibility. The fact that an elder had become the first woman moderator was something which a lot of the women ministers found difficult to accept because they were the ones who had had all the struggles and there was a woman minister who was nominated at the same time as me. It was three years after me that Sheila Kesting became the first woman minister to be moderator.

'By that stage I had realised that there were huge inhibitions in the Church to appointing women to positions of responsibility like that and that these were not worthy of what we said we were about because we had had women ministers and elders since the mid-1960s and here we were in 2003 and we still hadn't had anyone in the top job. And I also think that because of my ecumenical background I was beginning to realise that it was a double insult to women in other Churches who couldn't take positions of leadership that we were not stepping up to the plate effectively when it was possible for us. Elders are ordained as well in the Church of Scotland and in the various governing bodies you're supposed to have equal numbers of elders and ministers so there is a kind of joint responsibility between the ministers and the elders. So from our point of view it wasn't entirely surprising that an elder like me should be involved in this way [although the last one was in 1587].

'The moderator's role is to moderate the General Assembly for a week in May. You're up there chairing the debates and that's all the moderator did until the beginning of the twentieth century. At that time the tradition started of the moderator staying in post for the full year and spending the rest of the year going round visiting people and being a visible principal representative and opening doors for the Church. We were also assigned to one of the Armed Forces, in my case it was the Army, so I would spend three or four days down in the south-east of England with the army finding out about that. The army and the services in general are very conscious of the hard questions in life and so they're very appreciative of the role of the Church and they take that very seriously. And then there are overseas visits. I went to South Africa and India and to North America, Poland and the Czech Republic for shorter visits. In my case the Pope died during my year and I went to his funeral on behalf of the Church and I was the only Church representative there who was a woman, which was interesting. It was also the year of the tsunami and I was due to go to India just a few days after it had happened, so we saw and met people who were affected by that.

'In terms of being a spokesman for the Church as a moderator it's interesting that I had been the convenor of the Church and Nation Committee because in fact the Church has its spokesman there. When it comes to political matters the spokesman for the Church of Scotland should be the convenor of what is now called the Church and Society Council and in that role you build up relationships with journalists and with politicians and so there is quite a lot of close engagement happening and statements being produced very frequently. I was very conscious of the Church of Scotland being a broad Church and therefore having within it a whole lot of tensions. The tensions can be creative but of course if you're the person who's carrying the tensions it can be quite stressful and so one of the stresses I think is the difference between being very institutional and therefore faceless. There's a strength in not flying off the handle with celebrity but at the same time that institutional nature of the Church makes it very difficult to communicate the faith.

'The moderator's role is for a year but if you were moderator for more like four years you would have more of an executive role which you don't have at all now. You make no decisions as moderator and I think it's something which the Church of Scotland should look at. I think there's still a lot it could do even with the one year because if the rest of the Church councils were keyed up they could use the moderator as a spokesman or as a focus for concentrated activity. They didn't have a strategic approach to how the moderator could be used to serve their purposes better. There could also be an outward-facing role for the moderator, which is not just that of defending the positions of the General Assembly which is what the convenor of Church and Society does, but rather is about promoting an understanding of the Christian faith in Scotland.

'Having an institutional Church is fine in a society where everybody has a faith and knows what it is, but I think I was coming along as moderator and realising that a lot of the time what you were wanting to communicate with people was what it was like to be a person who believed these kinds of things. This was brought home to me in a conversation I had with the journalist Sally Magnusson early on where she was interviewing me and the interview wasn't going well and she said, "Look, Alison, I keep asking you these questions and you keep telling me what the Church thinks. I want to know what you think." Now that's quite scary when you're used to being a Church representative. So, yes, there's a tension there between these two and trying to personalise the Church of Scotland is a wider question than just what the moderator's role is.

'I think there are different ways of being the first woman in every walk of life. You can either show that you can do everything the same as the men do or you can show that it can be done in a different way and so the fact that I was both a woman and an elder made it easier for me to do things in a different way. As an elder I wasn't trained to preach and so I shouldn't have been going into the pulpit and preaching and I tried very hard to get ministers to find other ways of involving me. I tried to soften the role in various ways by what I was wearing and the way I would approach various issues.

'My husband of course was doing the same kind of job. I mean he was the first man who was the spouse of the moderator and so he was also coming up against expectations about the role and I think in some ways he managed this one better than I did. When we were in India people were astounded that a husband was following his wife around and I think he did quite a lot for that role there. He had a job as a merchant banker and he didn't give up his job for the year, so he saw himself as paving the way for ministers' wives or moderators' wives who were career women and couldn't easily give up their jobs. That also meant that on various occasions I used my chaplains a lot more than other moderators would do because I would need somebody to accompany me and they were important at the end of a busy day when you need to have somebody to offload to.

'When I was on Presbytery visits as the moderator I was often introduced to more of the caring professions and I was able to be involved in World AIDS Day with a specific focus on women and AIDS. I was very conscious that it wasn't so much what I did but the fact that I was a woman gave encouragement to other women to do things. Any effect that there has been of a long-lasting kind in the Church will be because people in their own congregations and in their own place in the Church were encouraged to do new things because there was a woman that was moderator.'

I suspect Alison underestimates the importance of her role as the first female moderator and I know she doesn't want it to define her. She was popular and since then two more women have been appointed to the role, most recently the Right Reverend Lorna Hood in 2013. Although Alison's background was not in ministry her conversations with women ministers would no doubt have revealed that it wasn't always easy for them. I had been told that a number of parishes in Scotland simply would not appoint a woman minister and it was not possible for the Church to force the issue since it is the congregation that makes the appointment. At the same time I knew of a number of women ministers who were very popular so maybe things were changing. I wondered how Alison felt about the issue.

'I have to say that my own experiences as a woman in the Church of Scotland have been good ones, but that doesn't mean that I don't realise that for a lot of women it's been very difficult. Of course I would not have been able to do what I did had not Mary Levison [who brought the petition for the ordination of women to the General Assembly in 1963] and various other women pioneered the whole role of women in the Church. She was carrying the banner for women's ordination and we were very conscious of her because she was an exceptional woman. It was because of her that women were ordained as elders in 1966 and ministers in 1968. Some people wrongly think that it's a double whammy if you're a woman and an elder and see you as a pioneer. In fact because of the strange nature of the Church it's much easier to slip in a woman elder than it is to slip in a woman minister because women elders are not a threat to the hierarchy. It's much easier for the Church to accept a woman elder as moderator than it is for them to accept a woman minister and if you look at Presbyterian Churches round the world that have had women moderators then generally they have been elders the first time rather than ministers.

'The Church of Scotland does value a very democratic approach to things and I suppose the petition was in the 1960s when women were being "liberated" in all kinds of different ways. The Church was heavily engaged with society so it didn't have the same tendency to see itself as separated from society and so if there were movements within the wider society for women to take on further responsibilities it was maybe more difficult for them to resist it. Obviously you can dig around and find biblical justification for why it shouldn't happen if you happen to be that kind of person but beyond that is the psychological barrier of being used to a certain kind of person preaching and administering the sacrament. Some people apparently find it difficult to have a woman, but I have no insight as to why it should be like that.

'I do think there are difficulties for ordained women in Scotland as being a minister is quite a lonely place to be. I think

Church members feel they can dump an awful lot on ministers and expect them to bounce back again and that is doubtless hard for many men as well, but maybe they have different coping strategies. Of course there will also be many cases where the woman is simply dismissed and not treated seriously and that will be difficult. It's hard to bring that relationship back to the proper secure working relationship which you're going to need with the people around you in the congregation. There are parts of the Church, of course, where they will not appoint a woman to a congregation even though they shouldn't be discriminating in that way. There are parts of the Church where they either still or certainly until very recently would not have any women as elders. For example, it's only recently that Glasgow Cathedral has had any women elders.'

'I was keen to get Alison's views on a subject close to my heart, the sense that the Church of Scotland is struggling at the moment and spends a lot of time managing decline. Too often I have seen meetings that focus on petty issues and of course the issue of gay clergy and gay marriage is also dominating discussions at a higher level, apparently at the expense of developing a vision for the future. Thankfully there are congregations that have been seeing tremendous growth by focusing on outreach and encouraging younger people to become involved.

'I think we've got used to the idea of a smaller Church but I don't think it's in a bad place. I mean it is facing big challenges, particularly with a lot of ministers retiring, but I'm conscious of a lot of good things that are happening. In our own congregation, for example, we're doing a lot of work on a local community project which is generating a great deal of energy. We're not an evangelical congregation in the usual sense of the word and so we don't have huge numbers coming along on Sunday mornings, but there's something that feels fairly secure about our own congregation just now and also about many others. However there are small congregations that are still clinging on to a past that has passed them by and that's difficult. A lot of people within the Church who can remember the glory days feel that it's all going to rack and ruin. There are also a whole lot of systemic difficulties in the Church. The Church is a very strange body and it's one which can do wonderful things, but it can also be a very difficult place for people to be and it's a place where a lot of people can be given the justification for doing fairly bad things. There are a lot of negative things about the Church which you begin discover as you are in it for longer.

'I suppose one of the things has to do with how power is exercised in the Church and in our own system. For example you have Kirk Sessions, which are the place where decisions are made about the congregation and these can become little fiefdoms in some cases. People who in the rest of their lives don't actually exercise an awful lot of power can do so there which doesn't make it a very healthy organisation.

'In 2004 when I was moderator I went to the assemblies of our own Church and other sister Churches and they all were saying much the same thing which was along the lines of, "We're beginning to turn a corner. We've got to the stage of accepting that we're not going back to the way things used to be." It was managing decline with a vision and there's more attention to what's happening locally rather than at national level and seeing value in other ways of being the Church. Having women does affect the power balance and anecdotally there's a big difference within the Assembly in terms of who is sitting there and who is speaking, and it's the men that do the speaking and it's the women who sit there in some debates but a lot of the women who did speak were the younger ones, so that's a good sign. If you are seen to be pushing yourself forward in the Church of Scotland then you're definitely shoved to the back of the queue and the men who manage to do it, do it very subtly. I remember once doing a talk about ambition in the Church of Scotland and it was very difficult work to do because, as I say, the general mood of promotion in the Church of Scotland is one where someone selects you.

'I think that having women in more roles in the Church will help on particular issues of social justice and again the Church of Scotland Guild, Scotland's largest Christian voluntary organisation, needs to be mentioned in this context because that is the continuing face of the women in the Church and they are a wonderful body that takes on very radical things such as taking a stand on things like prostitution and HIV much more firmly than the General Assembly would.

'It was interesting that the first Presbytery that I visited was the Western Isles. It's decided many years in advance which Presbyteries the moderator will go to in a particular year because clearly no one would have chosen the Western Isles for the first woman moderator. It was very interesting for me because I was expecting it to be difficult for people and I think it was for some. I started in Barra and went right up to Stornoway and in Barra I said to people, "Do people have difficulty with having a woman as moderator?" And they said, "Oh no, no, we don't mind, but wait until you get a bit further north." And so then when I got to Uist I said, "Do people have difficulty with a woman moderator?" "Oh no, no, no, we don't mind, but wait until you get further north." And so it went on until I got to Stornoway and they said, "No, we don't mind, why should we?" I'm not meaning by that to dismiss the difficulties which I think some of them actually did have, but they were also very hospitable and I think that the hospitality certainly won out and I had an excellent time in the Western Isles.'

Alison's experience as a woman in a senior role in the Church of Scotland had not been particularly difficult but I could sense her frustration at the restrictions put on the role of moderator. Many things might have changed if she had the freedom to develop the role, to speak out and to be there longer than a year. As it is the Church in Scotland may appear more friendly to women than parts of the Anglican Communion but I suspect most female ministers would still be aware of an undercurrent of prejudice against them. There may need to be a whole new generation of elders and even congregations before there will be complete acceptance across Scotland. Thankfully Alison was able to keep issues of social justice centre stage and to ensure the Church really engaged with society as a whole.

Favourite verse: Micah 6.8 '... and what does the Lord require of you but to do justice, and to love kindness, and to walk humbly with your God?'

Favourite woman: Martha. I think she gets a bad deal in the Bible. That ties in with the importance of the service side for me but also seeing that there's a spirituality about her as well, despite all her harassment in the gospel stories.

10

The Most Reverend Dr Katharine Jefferts Schori, Presiding Bishop

Katharine Jefferts Schori is the twenty-sixth Presiding Bishop of the Episcopal Church in America and 16 other nations across the world, with 2.4 million members. She was the first woman primate in the Anglican Communion and was the first woman to lead a major denomination in America. The Church is a province of the Anglican Communion [the gathering of Anglican and Episcopal Churches around the world with almost 85 million members in 165 countries, including the Church of England], led by the Archbishop of Canterbury. It has its roots in the Anglican Church but was formed as a separate entity after the American Revolution when America's Anglican clergy refused to swear allegiance to the British King. It also began as the State Church but no longer has that role. Katharine's role looks very similar to that of the Archbishop of Canterbury but she is keen to stress that it is less hierarchical and more about being 'first among equals'. She is officially the chief pastor charged with initiating and developing policy, speaking on behalf of the Church and visiting every diocese as well as speaking God's Word to the Church and the world. Her official seat is in Washington but her office is in New York.

Katharine is also an experienced pilot, an oceanographer, a keen runner, a wife and the mother of a daughter serving in the American Air Force and she has a number of honorary degrees. She is one of my more controversial interviewees and has suffered an astonishing amount of online abuse for difficult decisions that have been made during her tenure and even for particular sermons. A number of more conservative dioceses have broken away from the Episcopal Church and she has been blamed, even when these have been over long-term differences such as the issue of gay bishops. For many of her supporters her appointment simply enabled issues to appear that had long been bubbling below the surface. I was given very different impressions of her from both sides of the Atlantic, hearing that she was tough and difficult on the one hand and popular, warm, kind and down-to-earth on the other. I suspect some of the comments are more to do with differing personalities and outlooks.

I had no idea what I would find when I arrived at her offices on 2nd Avenue in New York. Her own office was like that of any chief executive but unlike most corporations there was a contemporary-looking chapel on the ground floor where Katharine leads a communion service on days she is in the city. As we started to talk I realised how some of the misconceptions about her could arise. Her naturally reserved demeanour gives an impression of a lack of warmth that soon changes as we get into conversation. I had been nervous about my meeting with someone of her stature but she also took a while to relax. She chooses her words carefully and is occasionally sensitive to mistakes, quick to tell me when I have mispronounced a word. Her natural reserve could be seen by some as a form of superiority but anyone who knows her well finds a very different individual who can be shy but has a tremendous concern for others and for issues that should concern the Church such as poverty, climate change and slavery. I began by asking how she became ordained and rose so rapidly to her position.

'I was a member of a congregation while I was in graduate school in Oregon. After my post-doc in oceanography ended there was a significant shift in federal funding for my research, which is very expensive to do. The bottom fell out in the mid-1980s largely because Reagan wanted to build Star Wars rather than devoting funds to basic research. It was becoming clear to me that if I wanted to continue doing oceanography I was going to spend most of my time writing grant proposals rather than doing basic science and at the same period, within a very short span of time, three people in my congregation asked me if I'd ever thought about being a priest. It had never crossed my mind. Women weren't ordained until after I graduated from university so I just never considered it and the short version of the story is it took me five years to say yes. I think they had probably seen leadership capacity in me and the willingness to keep digging spiritually, to keep asking questions, exploring, that kind of thing.

'The first woman priest was ordained in Oregon while I was a member of that church and she had been serving in the congregation. She'd been a deaconess for a long time and when deaconesses were regularised as deacons in the early 1970s she was among the first. And then there was a woman assistant in the church, newly graduated from seminary, who was also ordained in that congregation. It was in the aftermath of that that people began to ask.

'I was finally ordained in 1994 (at the age of 40) and I was called back to that same parish that had encouraged me to seek ordination. I was serving there half-time and I was teaching at the university and working as a hospice chaplain as well. I served my priestly ministry in that congregation and in others that were connected with it in the area and I helped to start a Spanish language congregation in that same place. I only served my last year there as a full stipend cleric.

'I was elected Bishop of Nevada in 2000. It's a little unusual that it was so quick. I was very interested in what in Britain is called non-stipendiary ministry. Here it's generally called Total Common Ministry, shared ministry. I was involved in getting it going in Oregon and I spent some sabbatical time in early 2000 driving across the western United States interviewing congregations and dioceses that were doing that kind of work. It was as a result of a consultation in Nevada that a priest said to me, "What you've done here is a lot like what a bishop does when a bishop visits. Can I put your name in the election process?" And I just laughed and said, "That's ridiculous," but it didn't let go of me and by the time I got home I realised that I was supposed to be part of the process. I felt called to go and help that diocese move into a new chapter of its engagement with that kind of ministry.

'Being a pilot helped make it much more realistic and easy for me to travel around. There is a great attraction – not to everybody, but I certainly found it – in being able to visit the variety of congregations and encourage and challenge people to grow in new directions, to examine the communities around them and to reach out into the communities rather than only focusing on their internal functioning and that was the big challenge with total ministry in that place. It was very internally focused.

'By the time I'd been a bishop for three years several of my colleagues in the House of Bishops began to ask if I would consider being part of the election process for Presiding Bishop and again I thought it was totally absurd, totally impossible. There was my gender and the fact that I was not from the east, all my predecessors had come from the east or the south-east, they'd been rectors of big congregations, bishops in big dioceses or had some international engagement. I just felt that it would be very unusual and unlikely but it didn't let go of me and they didn't let go of me and by the time it came due to assent to the process I was willing to say yes. I felt it was exceedingly unlikely, but I felt called to be part of the process.

'A vote is taken in the House of Bishops General Convention which is then consented to – one hopes – by the House of Deputies which includes the lay and clergy delegates from across the Church. There haven't ever been very many women involved. I was the ninth woman in this House of Bishops and by the time I entered at least one of them was retired.

'When it came to the vote I don't think it was purely my gender that was important. I think it was the fact that I was very interested in the international parts of the Church, in the immigrant parts of the Church and was willing to work in other languages and other cultures. I think that was a piece of it. The election was controversial for a handful of people. There were a couple of bishops who were very angry. They were angry when women were first ordained and felt that it was a threat to their authority and so one of them stood up the following day and said that he wanted alternate primatial oversight. He didn't want to have to pay attention to anything I might say. The reality is that the authority of the Presiding Bishop is rather different than it is in some parts of the Anglican Communion where the primate can direct bishops to do particular things. The Presiding Bishop in the Episcopal Church does not have that kind of authority. It is "first among equals". It's much more like the role that the Archbishop of Canterbury has with the other primates. It's a moral leadership and it's a visible role. To give an example, part of my job description is to visit every diocese of the Episcopal Church to preach and preside at Eucharist at least once during my term but I have to have an invitation in order to do that.

'The Presiding Bishop speaks to the world on behalf of the Church and speaks to the Church on behalf of the needs of the world and can issue pastoral letters and I do that periodically. There are governance rules in terms of presiding in the House of Bishops in the General Convention [the governing body of the Episcopal Church] when it meets as a whole every three years. I take order for the consecration of bishops and I've presided over almost all of them because I've felt that's been an important way to build relationships and collegiality. I do advocacy work on behalf of the Church and those who are not members of the Church. The connecting work, the bridge-building work, is an intrinsic piece of the work of any bishop and I think it's part of the ministry of every baptised person in some degree.'

One of the toughest aspects of Katharine's role must be dealing with the constant flow of criticism that comes her way, particularly online. I was shocked to see how many people who call themselves Christians are prepared to use language and behaviour that is often deeply hurtful. The Episcopal Church has seen a number of splits over various issues including the role of women and gay clergy which have led to a great deal of anger that is often focused on the leadership. There have also been financial challenges which make the job more difficult.

In June 2010 she was invited to preach at Southwark Cathedral in London which led to a barrage of criticism from the Church of England. It was seen as inflammatory at a time when arguments were going on about the role of women bishops in the Anglican Church. She could have come just as a priest but understandably she felt she was entitled to accept the invitation in her role as a bishop. It did not help her relationship with Rowan Williams but the end result was that she has become quite a heroine of the more liberal fringe in the UK. More recently she has been dealing with problems with the

Church in South Carolina and accusations have flown that she has acted 'above the law'. I wondered how Katharine dealt with all of these issues.

'That's the nature of leadership. The leader becomes a lightning rod and I think the challenge is to be non-anxious in the face of that. The issue of the split in the Church as a result of gay bishops is long past although some disagree and I understand it as another stage or another step in the deconstruction of patriarchal systems. I think it's been at least subconsciously responded to by patriarchal systems as resistance to men who appear to take a woman's role. I think that's where it comes from. In this country we wrestle with the place of African-Americans, with slaves, with women and children. We were one of the first provinces to invite the newly baptised of all ages to Communion and to say that you don't have to be confirmed in order to receive Communion and to welcome immigrants in what has largely been a white Church and gay and lesbian people. I don't know what the next group will be, but the nature of humanity says that there will be some other group who's not welcome. I think it probably has most to do with social class and economic status.

'I remember how bizarre it was when I was invited to come and preach at Southwark Cathedral. I'd been in Salisbury before the Lambeth Conference with all the Sudanese bishops and I'd been in a cope and mitre there, it wasn't an issue, but before I went to Southwark there was a directive of all things saying to the Dean that I was not to wear a mitre. It was just bizarre. I didn't want to put him in a very awkward position, but I was not willing to relinquish a symbol of my office. I cannot be who I am not. And so I decided to carry it rather than wear it. It was a staff member from Lambeth who had a bone in his craw about women bishops I believe, that's my understanding. In general I don't usually find that an aggressive response is helpful. I want to find a creative response that changes the conversation.

'When it comes to the issues in South Carolina you're probably aware that the leadership of five dioceses at this point have decided to leave the Episcopal Church – the four early ones were: San Joaquin, which is part of California; Fort Worth in Texas; Quincy, which is a very small diocese in Illinois; and

Pittsburgh, which is in Western Pennsylvania. This was overtly over issues of human sexuality related to the consecration of the Bishop of New Hampshire [Gene Robinson] a long while ago. South Carolina is the last one and it happened a year ago. Bishops said they were leaving and in Quincy's case the bishop retired and then much of the leadership of the diocese said, "We're no longer part of the Episcopal Church." There are two main issues. One is the status of the bishop who says he's gone. I have a role in helping the Church figure out how to deal with that or whether the bishop has "abandoned the Communion of the church", which is what our canons call one route or whether he has done something that contravenes some other part of the Church structure. In most of those cases we agreed that the bishop had abandoned the Communion of the Church and was no longer a bishop of this Church. It says nothing about the permanence of his orders, but he can't be a bishop representing this Church.

'The other issue is that in many of these cases the bishop and/ or clergy or members of congregations asserted that the property of the Episcopal Church was now theirs. Our canons are very clear that that's not possible and so it became my responsibility to say, "No, you cannot take the property with you, it's held in trust for the wider Church." That's the hard line that people complain about. I've been very clear from the beginning and two principles for dealing with the property are that we don't sell it to people who want to replace or displace or destroy the Episcopal Church as that's not an appropriate thing to do and we will sell it to other church bodies, but we expect a reasonable approximation of fair market value. We have to be good stewards. This is the bottom line. But, yeah, I've been seen as mean and nasty. My predecessor was less willing to be clear than I am and the situation was not as extreme. He did not have bishops leaving, but he wasn't as clear because the times were somewhat different.

'You can't deal with the online stuff very effectively. I call it discarnate communication. Face to face, most of us can find something to agree about and that's a starting place. I think that energetic conversation/dialogue is creative. We have the possibility or even the expectation that we will come to some place neither one of us anticipated if we engage it effectively.'

As Presiding Bishop, Katharine has become well known for her focus on poverty, diversity, climate change and particularly the Millennium Development Goals. In July 2010 she gave a powerful sermon at St Paul's Cathedral challenging a human system that denies the dignity of the poor, of immigrants, women, gays and Muslims and saying that "we lose our own dignity when we tolerate indignity for some". Remarks like these have tended to give her a label as a 'liberal' in America and I wasn't clear if that was a big problem in a country where politics dominates so many areas of life.

'Progressive is probably a more descriptive label than "liberal" if you're going to use a label at this point. We haven't arrived yet at the Kingdom of God, therefore we've got work to do, we've got to change, we've got to address the worst of the current realities. Our Church is pretty diverse. At our best we honour that diversity and understand it as a gift and a blessing. The echo in the political culture and climate at the moment is pretty awful because it's so fractured and there's such an unwillingness to negotiate or to make a common cause for the greater good. Our political system is nigh unto broken.

'*Shalom* is a Hebrew word, which is probably the closest approximation in one word for what we talk of as the reign of God. It means peace literally, but it means peace with justice because people are fed and housed and clothed and duly employed. It's a vision of what right relationship looks like. When the election process for this office began it became clear to me that the Church was really quite fractured over issues of human sexuality and to me it felt like navel-gazing. It's an important issue, but it's only one of a whole raft of things that we ought to be concerned about and it was focused internally. It was focused on internal church negotiation or arguing and my sense was and continues to be that we're called to move outward. Disciples of Jesus are sent to engage in God's mission, to produce something in this world that looks more like the reign of God.

'The Millennium Development Goals provided a framework, a focus for what a healed world looks like and what it looks like to move toward that kind of vision of *Shalom* and so I said that this is something we need to focus on as a Church. The goals are about the worst of human poverty worldwide but the biggest issue with them is that they're focused only in developing nations. The next iteration of development goals that will come from the UN and its conversation partners are going to focus more globally on what the right kind of development looks like, but they're focused on the least of these that Matthew 25 talks about, women and children. The last part of the goals talk about justice in terms of trade and economics and sustainable development on ecological and environmental issues. So it really constitutes a holistic picture of what the reign of God looks like in terms of the right relationship with human beings and the rest of creation.'

Women had played a crucial role in building the Episcopal Church in America and from the 1870s onwards had developed the Women's Auxiliary into a powerful force, raising substantial sums of money to fund the Church whilst leading the way on missionary work and social justice. However, when they tried to play a part in governance by asking for representation in the governing body, the House of Deputies, they were firmly rebuffed. At a similar time a black bishop was appointed but with unequal status, starting the interconnection between racism and sexism that was to be key for American women. In 1920 the Lambeth Conference in England agreed that women should be admitted to the lay councils of the Church but the Episcopal Church opposed it. The arguments tended to be less about theology and more about playing traditional roles. For the next few decades the battle continued until finally in 1970 women were allowed into the Church as unordained deaconesses. Unsurprisingly this was not enough for women and in 1974 a group of 11 women were ordained as priests in Philadelphia by several mostly retired Bishops. The House of Bishops was eventually forced to rule the ordinations valid, although against 'law and order' and from 1976 women could be ordained to all roles in the Church including that of bishop. The first female Bishop, Barbara Harris, was appointed in Massachusetts in 1988. Katharine recalled this time.

'It happened just as I was leaving college and I was not active in the Church at that point, so I had some dim awareness, but it didn't really register. I think it was important that it happened irregularly but authentically and those ordinations were regularised two years later after the Church had voted to agree. Our history of including women is really very odd. There was a Women's Auxiliary for a very long time which was a kind of parallel place for women to exercise leadership, but seating women as deputies was, you know, as bad as the race issue, "We can't have them in here. They'll pollute it or they'll hijack it." Just kind of astonishing.

'I think most people in the United States who think about these issues see a series of liberations or a series of struggles for full recognition and slavery had an immense impact in this nation and it still does. This is about mass incarceration as another way of controlling African-Americans and minorities. I think it's at the root of our immigration reform struggle at the moment. Race still defines much of the way this nation relates within itself and you can't understand the politics here without recognising that and when you begin to dig into it you see the pervasiveness of the issues everywhere.

'Women's suffrage happened in some of the States a little earlier. Wyoming – that bastion of liberalism which it isn't – was the first to admit women and to permit women to vote in State races, I think in the late 1800s, but national suffrage didn't happen until after World War I. There were women in Congress, there were women physicians, women in a variety of leadership roles in society, but they couldn't serve on vestries in the church in most places, they couldn't be lay readers in most places, they couldn't be deputies to the General Convention. A woman was seated for a while in the 1940s as a deputy but the men soon decided that there couldn't be any more women deputies and the first women weren't seated properly until 1973, which is abysmally late. I think the push to ordain women simply wouldn't wait. The year of 1973 was also the one that deaconesses were regularised as deacons.

'The ordinations in Philadelphia were in the same era that civil rights issues were so strong and much of it that was effective was non-violent. This was a non-violent way of asserting what needed to happen. I think it has to be understood in that larger context.

'Divorce had also been an issue across the Anglican Communion. It still is, even much more so in some parts of the

Communion, but I think we changed the rules here in the 1960s. I'm not even certain, but I've heard people tell stories about their parents being excluded from Communion when they were divorced and remarried. I had a personal experience of this as a child. A relative came to visit and the vicar of the church agreed to marry these relatives and my mother reflected afterward that the vicar had not asked whether either one had been married before, because if he'd known that one of them had been he would have had to get permission from the bishop and at that time it was very difficult to do. We still have that rule. In order to marry a couple in which one has been remarried you have to get a marriage judgement from a bishop. It's usually a formality, but it's still expected.

'I think some of the issues we're dealing with here in America are less about women in leadership than they are about decision making. States rights issues are also a piece of this. The sense of home control. That's clearly what's going on in South Carolina and they're explicit about it, "You can't tell us what to do." The General Convention makes a decision, the canons in every diocese have to agree with it but South Carolina says, "Sorry, we don't want to play. We're leaving."

'There's no theological difference in ordaining a woman as a priest and as a bishop. There's no distinction theologically which is what's so odd about the situation in England. When I was at the Lambeth Conference and in the Diocese of Salisbury we had a Q&A one Sunday afternoon with a group of members of the diocese and some man came up to me afterward and said, "Well, you know, I can tell you what the problem is. No man here wants to take orders from a woman." And I said, "Well, excuse me, the head of your Church is a woman and has been for 50 years and it's not the first time."

'When it comes to issues of gay leadership in the Church, it's a diocesan decision. Our General Convention has said that access to the discernment process for ordination cannot discriminate against people based on their sexual orientation. It's one of our canons adopted in the 1980s. It doesn't say we can require any bishop to ordain any particular person, that's not appropriate, but we can say that the access to the process has to be open. That was true for the ordination of women. There were still four dioceses that wouldn't ordain women. They were the four that wanted to leave eventually and eventually the leadership did, but I think in both cases it's about, "You can't tell us what to do."'

The consecration of openly gay Gene Robinson as a bishop was one of the most challenging issues that Rowan Williams had to face during his time as Archbishop of Canterbury. His desire to retain unity across the Anglican Communion made this particularly difficult for him. It was impossible for many Churches, particularly in Africa, to accept the situation. Although the consecration was before Katharine's time she was known to be supportive and has had to deal with much of the aftermath as well as the increasingly prominent issue of gay marriage.

'I think there was a great deal of surprise here that there was so much reactivity across the Communion. We've been talking about these issues since the early 1960s, for 50 years. We don't all agree still, but the collective discernment had come to the place where we felt that we were being led in a holy way to make this decision. Clearly other parts of the Communion aren't there. Some are. It's an internal decision. Decisions about consecrating women as bishops were being made locally. There'd been conversations about it in some places, but I don't think there was ever a formal decision. It was an awareness that it was going on and some places still don't ordain women at all.

'We're still struggling with the issue of gay marriage and we have not said yes to gay marriage in the Episcopal Church. We have said that there is local ability to sanction blessing unions and in jurisdictions where marriage is permissible then a bishop has pastoral discretion to be generous, but we haven't changed the canons about marriage, we haven't changed the prayer book about marriage – we may get there, but we haven't done it. The Anglican Church of Canada just at its Synod last week said that they're going to vote on this in 2016. They're clearer about it than we are. We're still discerning as a Church so I don't speak much about it. I'm very comfortable speaking about the need for the Church to bless people's lives in every way that it can, to promote ways in which people live holy lives. That's what we're about. If we get to the point of saying that we can celebrate a marriage for people of the same gender, all the better. But we're not there yet as a Church.

'There's an interesting book called *The Friend* by Alan Bray of the history in the Western Church of blessing friendships and it's a fascinating historical piece. The Western Church apparently did it pretty routinely from about the year 1000 well up into the 1800s, blessing two people of the same gender, blessing the vows they took to befriend each other. There are examples of knights buried in the same tomb. It was often called a "wedding" and observed in the same way that marriages were by making vows in the church porch and then going in and celebrating Eucharist. It's at least an image of what I think we're talking about. We're talking about a holy relationship that is a commitment for the rest of your life to support somebody else.

'We are an international Church in 17 different nations. We grew out of the United States part of the Church, and it's part of our colonial history largely, but the parts that are still part of the Episcopal Church need to be recognised and not dismissed as excess baggage. The issues that have fractured the US part of the Church have largely been non-issues in Latin America or in Taiwan, either because they're not present in the larger society or they're just not central to the way those parts of the Church understand their mission. They're much more focused on responding to the needs of the community around them which I've found really intriguing. There are women ordained in every part of this Church. The issue of gay marriage is on the radar, but it's not overwhelmed the rest of their understanding of mission in the way that it has in some parts of the US Church. In Honduras, Venezuela, Colombia, it just hasn't been an issue. Some of the difficulty in Africa is unfortunately due to exported conflict from Episcopalians or former Episcopalians who went and stirred things and continue to stir things for their own ends which is incredibly regrettable.

'I've been to every diocese in the Episcopal Church and I've been to probably half the provinces of the Communion. Where people are focused on other than themselves then the Church flourishes and it's when it's engaged in God's mission and not navel-gazing it thrives. Since I came into this role I see much greater engagement in outward mission than I did ten years ago.'

The role of Presiding Bishop seems to be a particularly challenging one for a woman with a family and many demands to travel. I understood that her husband had remained in Nevada and wondered how she managed to keep a life that was balanced and had a spiritual focus when the demands were so great and there seemed to be so many dramas to deal with on a daily basis.

'Well there are dramas in everyone's lives. From a spiritual perspective I've had to find a new rule of life at each stage of ministry and there's certainly coherence but the rhythm is different. I'm not in the same congregation every week. I'm not worshipping with the same people, preaching therefore is different. That's a process. It takes a while to figure out what that rule needs to look like in a new context. My husband is retired. He was a mathematics professor when I was elected Bishop of Nevada. He finished the academic year and retired. He said, "I've been a professor for 37 years, I can retire, so I think I will." It was a little early, but he's very happy doing what he's doing. He has a community in Nevada which he would not have if he lived here in New York because I'm only here five or six days a month. We get together every two or three weeks on the road. He will meet me at the next consecration in Virginia in ten days and then we will probably spend most of the summer together, so it works. I think it would be impossible for people who are newly married, but it works for us. My term ends in 2015 and there could be a re-election. It's never happened before. My predecessors have all served until they were retirement age, so I'm still trying to discern about that and I'm not certain. Whatever happens I don't think I will be able to retire and simply go read books. I've got a passion for this kind of reconciliation work.'

I left Katharine's office full of admiration for her courage and faithfulness in a very challenging role. I am not convinced that she hasn't been deeply hurt by some of the abuse she has received but her very visible sense of calling and her genuine passion for service must help. She is a woman of contrasts, tough yet kind, firm but also warm and inclusive and these strengths seem to make her ideally suited to her role. She captured the crucial importance of her public role so well when she told me that 'the biggest thing that women bring [to the Church] is the observable reality that there's a place here for everybody, that it's not just one kind of human being who is able to lead or speak or offer an image of God'.

Favourite verse: Isaiah 61.1 'The Spirit of the Lord God is upon me, because the Lord has anointed me; he has sent me to bring good news to the oppressed'.

Favourite woman: Well one of the examples I pull up frequently is the fact that Mary Magdalene is called by the Orthodox Church 'the Apostle to the Apostles'. If you want to talk about women's ordination that's where you have to start. She was the first witness to the resurrection.

11

The Right Reverend Chilton Knudsen, Assistant Bishop of New York

Meeting Chilton Knudsen, presently Assistant Bishop in New York, was a quite different experience from my meeting with the Presiding Bishop (Chapter 10). She is immediately warm, open and easy-going and it was easy to see why she was much loved in her previous role as the eighth Bishop of Maine. We met in the precincts of the late nineteenth-century Gothic-style Cathedral of St John the Divine which provides a wonderful haven from the bustle of the Upper West side of New York City. I felt totally at home sitting in her cosy flat looking over the well-kept gardens and hearing the sounds of happy children at the local day camp run by the Cathedral.

Like many women in the Church she went through some very challenging times but she has a good reputation for her ability to manage difficult issues without losing her humanity or sense of proportion. She was at college during the key period of student unrest in America as young people fought for civil, environmental and women's rights as well as protesting against the Vietnam War. She felt called to the Church long before the priesthood was open to women and announced her call as soon as the priesthood opened up to women in 1976. She participated in the consecration of the openly gay Bishop of New Hampshire, Gene Robinson, presided at his investiture and was the first female bishop to lead a prayer at the Lambeth Conference in Canterbury. Chilton has had a long-term interest in issues of addiction and recovery and of sexual misconduct in Church settings and has won awards as an outstanding women leader. She is married to Dr Michael Knudsen, a retired computer scientist, and they have a son who still lives in Maine. Since her

retirement she has been a missionary in Haiti. I asked her about
the impact of her upbringing on her life and her calling.

'My father was a Naval Officer and I lived all over the world
which is an important lens through which I see things. I grew up
an Episcopalian and wherever we were in the world we sought
out the Anglican Church. When I was back stateside living in
Pittsburgh, Pennsylvania while my father was making nuclear
submarines I felt a calling during my confirmation class. I was 11
years old and I asked the confirmation class teacher, "Why can't
women be ordained? It doesn't make any sense to me." Women
were beginning to be visible in the professions but he was so
upset. He called my mother and threatened that I wouldn't be
allowed to be confirmed because I was an upstart and I had
issues with my gender acceptance and all of that. I learned not
to talk about it except to very few people and anyway I thought
it was going to be a long way off. I was a young girl paying
attention to women moving into law and medicine and so on, so
I thought it was inevitably going to change one day.

'I did have a real sense that I was supposed to be a priest. I
had been sitting in the pew watching the priest do the things the
priest does and hearing people talk about him and I thought,
"I could do all of that." And that's when I asked that question.
It was a sense of calling and not just curiosity. I obviously was
not going to say any more, having had that kind of icy reply,
and then when I heard he had phoned to my mother I was very
clear that I was going underground. But I would talk about it
with a few people periodically. I had a lot of exposure overseas
to Roman Catholic Women Religious [nuns and sisters] because
that was often the only English-speaking school that we could
go to and again their sense of responsibility, running clinics,
hospitals and schools was an inspiration as well.

'So finally I started to train as a biologist and I was thinking
about medical school. I thought, "Maybe I'll just be very happy
if I'm doing a humanitarian thing like medicine," but in the
end I became a biology professor rather than going to medical
school. The tide changed here in about 1971 and finally after
three tries the Episcopal Church passed the ordination of
women. At that point I got on my knees and knew that I needed
to go to seminary, so the decision was made in the summer of

1976 and I entered seminary in September of 1977. I was aware of irregular ordinations and all of that but I didn't feel like I wanted to get that far out on the frontier. I'm sort of a next wave kind of girl.

'I became a deacon in June of 1980 and a priest in February 1981. Then I went to serve a small parish in the south-west suburbs of Chicago, a brand new place with lots of immigrant communities, Filipino particularly, and when you have one member of a Filipino family you have the whole family. Families began to come and we built a building.

'It was a very successful and wonderful time, although I was living in the Diocese of Chicago where people still made a great to-do about sitting on the opposite side of the aisle from us women. They would go to the other side of the Communion rail if one of us was administering the chalice and boycott the service if one of us was celebrating. That happened repeatedly over and over again from about 1981 until the mid-to late 1980s but this was mainly in the larger diocese. The actual church I was in was a small, growing struggling middle- to lower-middle-class church, full of immigrants and people with a real open mind. I have to hand it to them as I was the first woman to have charge of a congregation in the State of Illinois and they were lovely. They sort of pulled alongside and thought of me as the underdog they could support. By the time I left to take a diocesan position the tide had changed. Frank Griswold had been elected Bishop of Chicago in 1987 [later Presiding Bishop from 1997–2006] and he came in with a set of clarities, one of which was that women will be mainstreamed and he would call a senior woman to his staff. That was me.

'This was diocesan work in all its rich variety. Everything from one day you're talking to a priest who's in deep, deep trouble to the next day you're blessing a new building to the next day you're planning an important conference, all of that. I just ignored any issues about being a woman. We had a number of people who were very supportive with whom we could go and express our frustration, but I just focused on the people who did receive my ministry, who wanted to participate in it. I really don't need to convert anybody, I just want people to let me do what I'm called to do. I wasn't dealing with all sorts of heavy-duty anger issues or what have you, but I'm much more practical and so I got consumed with just doing a good job.

'During this time the Civil Rights Movement was paralleling or proceeding by maybe a decade depending on where you stand when you look at these two trajectories, but they definitely had a parallelism and of course now we have a third parallel which has to do with the gay and lesbian community. Who knows who will be next? But as somebody said, "The arc of human history bends toward justice." I found myself using a lot of the metaphorical language that Martin Luther King used such as, "Here I stand, I can do no other" or finding my own metaphors for the experience. I had that sense of conviction about what's right as opposed to what makes everybody around you happy, you know? It's very much what you have in your previous book, *Turning Points*. It takes courage, it also takes companionship and your stories over and over again point to the mentor or mentor context in which people were able to make a change. It speaks to all kinds of transformative experiences and the discovery of one's vulnerabilities by people who are important and willing to help.

'In my case I had all that. I continued my connection with Roman Catholic Women Religious and one of them became my spiritual director, eventually directing me on the 30-day Ignation retreat. I also had support from some Protestant women and by that time other Churches were ordaining women such as the UCC, Methodist and Presbyterian Churches. However I was really the first wave in Chicago so I didn't have a role model in place who was visibly exercising priestly ministry at a high level but I connected with women who were in other parts of the country, including here in New York, where as soon as it was legal, women were absolutely mainstreamed.'

Clearly the pressures on Chilton were immense, even if she could make light of them now. Chicago had been a particularly difficult place to be one of the first women priests, even with the support of the bishop. I knew that she had been treated for alcoholism and wondered what impact that had on her life and choices.

'I think the pressure for me is that I'm a bit of an over-achiever. The pressure was to really make my church just the best, strongest church in the whole diocese because everybody was watching and expecting me to fail. That's part of living in a climate with even veiled sexism. People are surprised if things go well. And things were going well and in order to sustain that pace and deal with the sadness I felt inside about our son, who is a special needs child, I turned to alcohol.

'My son was three when I entered seminary and he was four when he was diagnosed with a progressive neurological condition called Tourette's syndrome and he had a very bad case of it. In order to medicate the symptoms to some kind of sociable acceptance we had to medicate him way too much, so we did the trade-off and backed the medication off and helped him adjust to the social pressures when a person's different. I was determined to just keep going with a supportive husband and a good community of neighbours. At the time my parents were alive and they were both supportive, so you do it because other people help you. But that was a crushing kind of intensity – dealing with those two things together – and I recognised, thanks to some help from some very straightforward people, that I was getting in trouble with alcohol. I hadn't had that low point that people have where they really have lost so much, but I was able to use AA [Alcoholics Anonymous] and put myself in the care of some good, tough, strong, seasoned people. With the help of the 12-step programme and counselling I can say, "thank you God, sobriety's wonderful." My son is now 38 years old and he lives on his own in Portland, Maine. He's a janitor at the YMCA. We provide a little gentle oversight. We do his cheque book, we come down to his house and make sure he's thrown away food that might be spoiled, just sort of helping as we can.

'One of the things that every addict has to work on as soon as you've decided to make the move and get clean and get sober is about helping others. If you are a religious figure with some public visibility, suddenly everybody thinks you've hung out your shingle but during early recovery it's not good to focus on other people. I was helped by my counsellors and by my AA friends to say, "I'm not in business yet. I need to get more ground under my feet." But after a while I realised these problems are everywhere. They are everywhere in the Church and so I published a book called *So You Think You Don't Know One: Addiction and*

Recovery in Clergy and Congregations, with a woman priest who's also in recovery. She's been a long-time friend and we said, "We need to just tell the world some of what we're finding and see whether any of that makes sense to anybody."

'In Chicago, as soon as I took office working as Frank Griswold's pastoral care officer in 1987, it was as if a backlog of people had been waiting to have a receptive set of ears at the diocesan level around issues of abuse and sexual misconduct. There's a lot of secret-keeping, which is what everybody did in those days, and as a result not delivering good care to victims, so I soon found them ringing my doorbell. At that point I decided I needed to acquire some expertise so I started taking lots of training. It was absolutely in response to the flood at my door. At this point the Church was beginning to pay attention to these issues because big insurance claims were arriving and the Church began to feel the real pinch of that as people were coming back and asserting their legal rights.

'I think clergy and congregations particularly live in a set-up that enables that sort of thing to happen. Clergy have a kind of unguarded intimate access to people. People have a sort of unguarded hunger for God and that's why they're on your church doorstep and they confuse that with the erotic hunger for connection with other people. It's a confusion that's been around as long as we've had spirituality and also because priests are usually not accountable in some way. They could go over and have lunch in the home of the sad divorcee or the bereaved widow and nobody would wonder about that, although they probably do now. And I also think priests sometimes get confused about how we are seen by other people. We feel friendly towards them. They feel a complex set of dependencies and projections and imaginings and yearnings and so clergy are not always attentive to how complex someone's feelings are when they're interacting with a member of the congregation.'

Chilton eventually moved on from Chicago to become the eighth Bishop of Maine in 1977. She was the first female bishop there and only one of eight female bishops across America. New England has since been seen as one of the more liberal areas of the Episcopal Church, with the appointment of the first female Bishop Barbara Harris in Massachusetts in 1988 and the first openly gay Bishop Gene Robinson in 2003. However it was still a challenging time for Chilton to move into such a role and I was curious why she felt drawn to it.

'When I was working as part of the diocesan staff at the Diocese of Chicago I watched Frank Griswold take on the ministry of a bishop because I was with him from the beginning. As I watched this very talented, very sincere and earnest guy wrestling with this vocation I began thinking, "You know, I think I would like to do this too." I accompanied him on lots of occasions and he delegated a lot of things to me. He gave me lots of areas to deal with where I had to make my own judgements and I discovered lots of times that they were good judgements, my instincts were sound and I found a real gratification in working with a system. And not just the smaller system of the parish which after the third or fourth year of trying to get Sunday School teachers and having people resist it just gets a little boring for me. Of course I have nothing but admiration for people who year after year can bring fresh insight and energy within the same parish setting. My growing up years were much more rich and sort of richly textured and I think I get bored easily.

'My leadership skills were affirmed over and over again by getting national positions and responsibilities such as becoming a trustee of the Church pension fund. It was also a very complex organisational challenge having leadership of the diocesan level and national leadership as a trainer in this whole emerging area of responding to sexual misconduct in a way that's pastoral and fair and appropriate given that we're a Church. We're not a legal system, we're an ecclesiastical body.

'I was the first woman Bishop in Maine and it was a big thing for them to choose me. I had been a nominee in other elections before. I had gone to the almost ballot level several times and all of those situations were very affirming. In one case they couldn't get the gender thing in their heads and in another case I was way too liberal for them about controversial issues. The explanation was pretty easy to understand. The Diocese of Southern Virginia said, "You are wonderful, you have all the skills we need but you are way too liberal about gay and lesbian issues for you to work here." In one place they said, "Our diocese isn't ready, but ... " and here's where the affirmation comes, "in conversing with you, checking your references, reading things you've written it's very clear that you're called to be a bishop but just not here." For me it's a funny message of affirmation and acknowledgement basically coming from of a kind of backwardness.

'I had been a nominee in Western Massachusetts before Maine and I was not elected there, but again I heard the same things, "We want to call our favourite son, but we really want you to know we see good things in you." When Maine put me on the ballot I was ready to say, "This running for bishop is tiring, I just have to take some time off. I do believe I'm called to that ministry, but I can't keep doing this." However I read the profile for the Diocese of Maine and it sang to me, particularly because the previous bishop had resigned under pressure because of multiple sexual misconduct issues, so I thought I would have something to bring to the table here in terms of healing. I read the profile and realised it would be perfect. People around the Church would call me or write me and say, "You would be perfect, but Maine is too conservative, they won't call a woman." Well Maine is actually not conservative. Maine has two federal senators who are women. Half the colleges in Maine have female presidents, female directors of medical staff. It's a matriarchy. Why? Because in the old days the guys all went out to fish, that was Maine's economy, so they're away for months at a time and women are the people running the town and running the school and so on, so it was a sort of prejudice people expressed. Maine was wonderful.

'So I got elected and three churches out of the 68 of them in the diocese said, "You can't come here being a bishop. You can come be the manager of the diocese, but don't lay hands on our children in the Sacrament of Confirmation." I'm gently stubborn so I said, "That's fine. We'll arrange for a bishop to come in and do all that, but you will not ignore me, you will not sideline me, I will come to the harvest supper, I will give the meditation for the lantern series, we will do that. We will be in connection. I'm the Bishop here. I won't force my Sacramental Ministry on you, but I am going to exercise this ministry." And within a year all three of them were totally fine. They went through a process of working on it and it helped that I said, "I'll give you all kinds of room right now to have another bishop, but we're going to connect." As we connected I think some people found they had been holding prejudices that were not realistic. So everybody's fine. In fact all three of those churches now have either called a woman to be their rector or sponsored a woman for holy orders.

'I can't tell you there weren't moments that I wasn't angry, but I saw that what worked was sustained attention, caring relationships, the honest opportunity to relish our differences, not to need to change each other but to find points of connection and commonality. After a while it's OK and it just takes that kind of patient work, so to tie two pieces of my life together I think that it helped having a special needs child where progress is very slow, where you have to keep your pressure consistently up, where you can't let emotions dominate the way you interact with that person. You have a sense that he's going to figure out after a while how to take the train, he's going to figure out how to get to his locker in the morning and get the books he needs for the next classes, we just have to kind of keep patiently working with him on that and it was the same for this issue in the Church.'

One of the most well-known incidents in the recent history of the Anglican Communion was the consecration of an openly gay priest, Gene Robinson, as Diocesan Bishop of New Hampshire in 2004. It was a momentous occasion but not without its risks for him as apparently he had to wear a bullet-proof vest at the consecration. It proved to be a major challenge for the Archbishop of Canterbury as he did his utmost to retain unity across different parts of the Anglican Church across the world. It has always seemed surprising to me that this event could have happened in a country that has some of the most conservative congregations, stridently against issues such as women in leadership and climate change. However America is genuinely a land of contrasts and New England has always had a character of its own. Chilton was at the heart of this event, presiding over the service.

'When you're consecrated you're ordained to the holy order of a bishop. When you're installed you're put into your office as the bishop of the diocese, so Gene was consecrated a bishop by Presiding Bishop Frank Griswold, but when the time came for the bishop he was succeeding to hand over to him I presided at that service. I was the president of the Province of New England. Other Anglican jurisdictions would have labelled that role as Archbishop but we don't use that term.

'I could have had someone else do it but I couldn't be more proud to be there and so there are lots of pictures of me presiding at that service with Gene circulated in the Associated Press, Reuters and even the BBC. It inflamed a few people back home in Maine and upset them, but again we went around and said, "Let's just sit and talk. You don't have to change your mind. I'm not here to make you think like I do, I just want to keep the space open for all of us to feel like we belong." Some people left, but I think we diffused a lot of the anxiety with those conversations.

'There was lots of unhappiness, sadness, anger. I guess my father being a Naval Officer taught me a lot and living and growing up in the Service gave me a perspective. As we say in the Navy, "You salute the office, not the person." The office is established for the mission of the organisation. It's not because of personality issues and so if the office of bishop has to do with leading, teaching, sacramental ministry, administrative oversight, pastoral care, then the question is the qualifications not the sexual orientation. For me, to allow one's sexual expression to dominate all those other things is in fact heresy. You know, inept, incompetent, bumbling heterosexual people are eligible for this on the basis of their sexuality, but not competent, gifted, talented people who might be gay or lesbian, so I just feel like it gives an exaggerated weight to one part of a human life over all the other things. So I've always had a liberal outlook and there've been gay and lesbian people in our life and in our family for as long as I remember. So I was proud of the Church that did the right thing, in spite of the resistance and push back and the inevitable penalties that would follow. That we went ahead and made the right decision even with the pressure of people saying, "You're going to make people unhappy." People are unhappy already, you know.'

Chilton has played significant roles in the last two Lambeth Conferences in 1988 and 2008. The conference takes place every ten years at the invitation of the Archbishop of Canterbury and is the key opportunity for bishops across the Anglican Communion to gather together. In 2008 Rowan Williams had a difficult challenge to preserve unity over the issue of consecrating gay clergy and to ensure that there was more than one focus for the media. He blamed the North American Churches for threatening the unity of the Anglican Communion and asked for a moratorium on the consecration of gay clergy and same-sex blessings. Not surprisingly Bishop Gene Robinson was not included, as invitations can be withheld from bishops who have caused division, but I remembered hearing him on the radio in London during that week as he visited England in a private capacity. My impression was that Rowan was considered to have done a good job in difficult circumstances but I am not sure whether Chilton would agree.

'I was a brand new bishop in 1998 and went to the Lambeth Conference. I participated in the prayers of the people and that was a very deliberate intentional thing. The liturgy committee wanted to put a female bishop in a particular role. You couldn't have a theological objection about leading the prayers of the people. How can you object to that? I'm not presiding at the altar, I'm not pronouncing a blessing, but it sure did get tongues wagging.

'I was back there again in 2008 and I watched the process of "intentional dialogue". I was a facilitator. I took all the training and it's a set of skills I was glad to brush up on and strengthen. We had come to significant consensus in every group about what it meant to live together and it included that we would not "do jabs" at each other. We would not take advantage of the public platform to lob a passive-aggressive derisive remark to people of another opinion. We would not ascribe hostile motives to people who felt differently. We would expect charity all around and then Rowan violated that. He was in the room when we agreed to those principles, but he took the opportunity at the last service to kind of drop a bomb. The sermon was very much affirming people for what they've done and so on and so forth and then there was a bomb he kind of lobbed in near the end about the fact that the Americans and the Canadians and others were not honouring the will of the majority and were doing renegade things. I just remember the feeling that swept over the cathedral when he did that.

'So after that I found a number of people of every opinion

and said, "What did you think of that last comment from him?"
Even people who are of the mind to be suspicious of change and
resistant to change felt that was just a misuse of the privilege
of the pulpit. You don't excoriate one body of people from the
pulpit to win points with the other body. And so I was sorry that
happened because it was going well and I refused to give that
one misspeak the power to erase all the good that was done, but
for me I had to name it and so when I was interviewed I said, "I
really regret that comment because the spirit was moving in such
a clear way, everybody was feeling it. We're going to be able to
live with these differences," and he was doing fine, his sermon
was full of hope and affirmation and then that happened.

'I felt enormous disappointment and sadness and I guess I
felt some anger, although that wasn't the predominant emotion.
I saw somebody who was really trying hard and earnestly and
just simply couldn't get out of his own way. When you see that
you deeply regret it and you just feel so terrible for the way the
person was just full of grace and all of a sudden when the final
grace note could have been sung they went into a minor key.
So I did talk to him about that. I have had other encounters
with him where we haven't discussed it again, but I did say,
"I thought you were doing such a beautiful job bringing it all
together, helping everybody feel like they belonged in the same
church, in the same room, in the same spiritual reality and then
I want you to know how I heard you and I'm not the only one."
And he said in a kind of vague and scholarly way, "Well, you
know, probably it was not the best thing to say at the time," or
something like that.'

Although Chilton doesn't like to think of herself in the
forefront of the fight for the ordination of women she was
around at one key stage of the battle, the 'irregular' ordination
of 11 women priests in Philadelphia by three bishops before the
General Convention had authorised the ordination of women
clergy. It was hard to imagine women going that far in the
Church of England and I wondered if she felt that had been a
necessary step.

'I think they were just like the civil rights marches in Alabama
in 1965 and the occupying of the national Capitol steps. It
didn't break any law because the final interpretation of it had

not been made, so in my view it was irregular but not illegal. We use the term irregular ordinations because the text that says "he" was never specifically interpreted to mean "he – male" as opposed to the generic version of mankind. So I thought, "This is very gutsy and it elevates the question." People have to pay attention to this kind of elevation the way they paid attention to Martin Luther King. They didn't just sit back and say, "What a shame that all these little girls have been killed, it's too bad and the sheriff was using a hose on protestors and they're getting hurt," but instead went and spoke in the public square, so I think it was right. The women spoke not so much with their words but with their actions. It was a kind of non-violent civil disobedience.

'It was part of the great tradition of civil disobedience which really emerged from labour management stuff in the place where I was, which was Chicago. I just saw it as something that was inevitably going to happen. I wouldn't have been one of those woman myself because I'm just not a frontier person, I'm a backup, but I was very happy when it happened and I knew the next time we have a General Convention the question will be called and I hope we make the right decision. So in 1976 we did and of course it included bishops as one of the Holy Orders. In an established religion it's a little trickier with bishops because certain public privileges attend to the order of ministry such as being Members of the House of Lords, so they have civil responsibilities as well. In order to get the work done of passing the legislation ordaining women as priests in the Church of England, they said, "OK, we'll take priest and deacon now and we'll deal with bishop later," recognising that it was a very different problem given the established religion.

'Now it took a while for a woman to be elected as a bishop in America between the priesthood in 1976 and Barbara Harris's consecration in 1988. In her case you can mix in there the gender issue but also mix in the cultural issue around authority belonging to women. However holistic our view of holy orders the "authority" of a bishop is understood even at an unconscious level and so "promoting" a woman to that level of authority is a very different thing from calling a woman to be your parish priest who's going to hold your hand at your bedside and baptise your children. The fact that the first woman was from New England which is known to be very progressive and that it was a woman of colour and a woman who was a suffragan, which is a subordinate bishop role, did soften that sense of authority.

'It was a bold gesture on the Diocese of Massachusetts for them to elect a woman. Women had been on the ballot before but never elected and for them to elect this talented, strong, competent woman was wonderful. She took a huge amount of heat and pressure and it was all about her never having had a parish of her own, that she didn't go to seminary, she passed all her exams but she didn't do the usual track and that she was divorced, so people used those codes to complain about the fact that she's also female and black. I think a number of people recognised that going to the public ear with complaints about her being female and black was so politically incorrect you weren't going to do it. So it was things like her having long painted red fingernails and that they're a distraction when she's at the altar and that she's divorced. She has a corporate background and she worked for an oil company in the PR department. So those were the stalking horses for the other objections.

'I think the splits in the Church are wonderfully cleansing and like pruning a vineyard to use a scriptural image. I remember House of Bishops' meetings when we still had the unhappy, angry, distressed, separatist kind of bishops in our midst and, to be honest with you, it's hard to be open and candid when you know that somebody's going to be quoting you to the nearest microphone. During that period of time from say 1998 to 2005 or 2006 before the split really split it was an awfully difficult time to have a sense of community as bishops because we really did have all of these press and media people sticking microphones in front of the faces of unhappy people because they just love to print unhappiness. The issue of Gene Robinson was the precipitant but a lot of people had been distanced before around gender. The dioceses that left the Episcopal Church, except for Pittsburgh, had all forbade the ordination of women when it was approved, so it was just simply a kind of straw that broke the camel's back. I actually think the Church is very much stronger now.

'I think Katharine [Jefferts Schori, Chapter 10] has done what she has had to do and in the face of people all tugging on her sleeve asking her to "make nice" or wishing that she would somehow cave in to various pressures. I think she's extremely strong. I think she has a profound interior life like a lot of introverts do, which helps her when the pressure is on to be very firm and not to cave. I think she's tired also. It's been a tiring thing for her. She's helped enormously with the people who are open to women in positions of strong leadership because she has succeeded in so many ways.

'I think the people who are going to raise the biggest objection to issues like gay marriage have already left. I think there are some people who have had to concede over and over again that this Church isn't going to be exactly like I want but I'm loyal and I've got a context in which I can function comfortably and so they stay. And the Episcopal Church doesn't feel to me like it's always on the verge of splitting. It lives with a significant amount of tension and the tensions that led to the splits in 2004–6 when Gene was the issue of the day, those tensions were there for a long time. They weren't just about Gene. They were about all kinds of other stuff, including the ordination of women, the preparation of a new prayer book and all of that.

'Younger people respond to three things in the Episcopal Church. One is the sense of mysticism around a rich sacramental life. They're drawn to the service, the incarnational feeling we have that Christ is out there waiting for us to help put food on people's plates and a roof over their heads and thirdly these younger folks like that we're a community of diversity. They like to see that there's a partnered gay man at the altar. They're happy to see that the Hispanic woman is exercising her ministry. This is a generation of folks from about I'd say 30 on down and they're not having any truck with all of this itchiness. We have a bunch of young people doing things. In fact over in Staten Island there's mission groups of young people rebuilding houses as we speak. I think that's how they pray. I think you go through a phase in your life where what's going on inside is so complicated – it has to do with relationships and autonomy and independence and sexuality – it's just hard to have an interior life in the middle of all that, but you can sure go and put food on tables or help rebuild houses and I think that's how they pray.'

Favourite verse: Luke 7.47 'Therefore, I tell you, her many sins have been forgiven – for she loved much' (NIV).

Favourite woman: The woman who knelt at Jesus' feet and washed them with her tears and anointed him with perfume in Luke 7. Sometimes she's anonymous, a woman of the street or a woman of questionable reputation. There was something so overwhelming about her recognition of who Jesus is and her attention to his pastoral needs, having been out on dirty roads. I just love the feistiness of that and her willingness to be visible in a compromising situation. The story also speaks to me too about serving others even when people are critical. Luke sees that women are in positions of intimacy with Jesus and he is affirming of them.

12

Helena Kennedy, Baroness Kennedy of the Shaws, QC

One of the great pleasures of writing this book is the chance to meet women I have admired for some time. Helena Kennedy is certainly in that category. She was born in Glasgow and has remained a popular figure in Scotland, although she hasn't lived there for many years. For me, there is something typically Scottish about her work as an advocate and social reformer, championing civil liberties, education and human rights and giving a voice to those who have the least power. Her upbringing in a Roman Catholic and socialist family and as part of a tight-knit working-class community in Glasgow clearly informs much of her work as a barrister and she can often be heard on the radio fighting injustice in many different forms.

When you read Helena's CV it is hard to imagine how she also has time to be a wife and mother to three children. She is active as a life peer in the House of Lords and as a QC [Queen's Counsel], chairs numerous boards, writes books and judges book prizes, presents programmes, is a patron of several charities, has her own Foundation focusing on widening partici-pation in higher and further education and is the Principal of Mansfield College, Oxford. She has come a long way from the Glasgow tenement where she grew up and has had her own sense of being an outsider as she made her way through the very male world of the legal establishment and fought particularly challenging and emotive public cases, including the Guildford Four appeal.

I had heard Helena express her views on the refusal of the Catholic Church to ordain female priests and was intrigued that she could reconcile her Catholic faith with her own passion for equal opportunities for women. She had said that her father had taught her to stand up for her beliefs, however painful that might be, and she had clearly decided that included the Church. She signed the Catholic Scholars' Declaration in 2012, joining an international group of theologians and academics in saying that the faithful have suffered from 'misguided' church rulings on sexual ethics and including a section on women in the priesthood.

I met Helena in the House of Lords. She is a friendly, attractive and well-dressed woman with that aura of efficiency and focus that clearly enables her to juggle so many balls in the air. We discussed her upbringing and the importance of religion to her whole family as well as the sense that injustice must be fought. She is clearly passionate about the impact of the Catholic Church's teaching on women.

'I was brought up in a family that were both Catholic and socialist. And there was that combination of feeling that you were responsible for people around you and that, in creating a better life, you wanted it for other people too. All of that came from my parents, who were truly good people and also from the community I lived in and the school that I went to, because that was the ethos all around us. And we didn't have that idea that you only looked after number one and that money was a god. I think my mother had a very strong sense that nobody was better than us and therefore my mother would have bowed to nobody and I've got that too, I can't do deference. I got that particularly from her, that you don't tug your forelock to anybody. But the corollary of that was that you don't treat people as lesser than you. And the idea that you would be dismissive of people because they were stupid or because they were poor or because they were feckless would have been absolutely unacceptable to my parents. That's ground deep into my being too and I think it's a very Scottish thing. Although we were Catholics, we were affected by the Presbyterian tradition too, which is much less hierarchical, it's about flatter structures and I think that I breathed that in, that sense that we're all "Jock Tamson's bairns" [a popular saying in Scotland] meaning that there is no difference between us. And so I think that being Scottish and a Catholic is an interesting mix with the added impact of Presbyterianism.

'In recent times, because I had publicly said that I supported women in the priesthood, I began to receive communications from women who quite clearly have a vocation and would make wonderful priests. It's a great source of pain for them not to be able to play that role. These are people who are far more religious than I could ever be, who are far more committed to helping others in their spiritual fulfilment and it just seems to me that it's wrong. I've seen this over the years. I remember as a child the business of women coming to my mother for help. I remember distinctly a woman whose husband had beaten her and my mother going into a drawer and finding some money and giving it to her because the woman had no place to go. My mother told her to go back to her parents and helped her to do that.

'I also remember people in unhappy, miserable marriages who went to priests. I was a great observer and listener, I was the child in the corner who read the book but while I was reading the book I was also listening in on grown-up conversations. And I remember people confiding in my mother about the misery of their marriages and going to the priest and being told that that's what the Catholic Church expected of you, that you stayed in wretched, miserable marriages in which you were abused. One of my mother's cousins was abandoned by her husband. She met somebody else and yet was seen as a 'scarlet woman'; she wasn't able to remarry and couldn't receive the sacraments. The cruelty of it all was terrible with regard to women. So we've got to remember those stories and remember that in some parts of the world women are still leading those kind of lives. In parts of Latin America that teaching still continues and women think they have to stay in those kinds of marriages.

'I remember coming down to London when I'd just qualified as a barrister and been called to the Bar and one of my women friends who was a Catholic had married young. She was a little bit older than me and she'd married and had a baby and she was a very upper-class girl. Her marriage broke down and I remember Mary was able to get an annulment, although she had a baby. And I remember realising that it really was about who you knew and about making the canon law [in the Catholic Church] work for you in the way that it worked for the Princesses of Monaco or members of the Kennedy Family. If you were sufficiently well-connected, marriages could often be dissolved in a way that was not possible for ordinary folk.

'And because I had moved into a world where there were many privileged people, I saw the differences in the way the Church dealt with different people. And I feel very strongly that women have been hugely short-changed. And, although we've all moved on, one of the terrible things is that it leads people into a double life in which they hear the teaching on things like contraception, IVF, stem cell research, the whole business, and they all hold views totally at odds with the teaching of the Church but they just somehow find a way of ignoring it and just go about their business being Catholics in their own way.

'If there were women priests in the Catholic Church I think they would be much more compassionate about the struggles that women have around things like contraception. I am a patron of a project in central London, Women of the Well, that works with women that have become prostitutes, women who have often come from abusive homes, domestic violence, sexual abuse, horrible stuff, and have dependency then on drink and drugs. The nuns who work with them are the most remarkable women. The nuns who are at the front line working with the poorest know sometimes that those women will make choices which their lives force upon them. And the idea that they would be saying to them, "You're a disgrace because you've had an abortion" is just impossible. They know that sometimes women have very, very hard decisions that are forced upon them because of the lives that they lead. The nuns are, of course, all in favour of reform in the Church. I also know from nuns who have worked in Africa, particularly in the field of health, that they wouldn't dream of saying to people that they can't use condoms. And most of the priests wouldn't dream of it either because they see the effects of HIV and AIDS on families and on children and so forth. And the burden of course is so often carried by women. And so the teaching on that, as far as I'm concerned, is wrong. And I think that to be saying the answer to this is not to be having sex at all is really cruel. And I think that many of the people on the front line just get on with it and ignore the teaching.

'I think that when women take on priestly roles they will be as varied as the kind of priests that we have. We have this conversation about whether women as judges do it differently. And the answer is that some of them do but it also changes the nature of the judicial discourse. If you've got women there then the conversations become different and you learn from each other. And I think that having a woman on our Supreme Court has been hugely beneficial to women but we've only got one and that makes me very cross. But it has made a big difference because I can point to a number of different cases where there has been a woman's voice to say, "Hold on a minute, how does this impact on the real lives of real women?" Women can talk about the effects of female genital mutilation and whether it should be a basis for somebody claiming asylum. And there's no doubt that having women participating in those sorts of discussions makes the difference and can often change the nature of the debate.

'It's not to say that you don't have wonderful men making the difference for women. And some of the men who've really helped change the legal profession and who made allies with women like me were very important to it. And it will be men, as much as women, who will end up changing the Church.'

Helena was a powerful force in promoting equal opportunities for women in the law, whether as lawyers, defendants or victims and received a lifetime achievement award from *The Times* in 1999 for her work. I could see that her passion for the subject could be very useful to the women arguing for the ordination of women in the Catholic Church but was more surprised to see that she had become involved in the debates in the Church of England, both for the ordination of women priests in the 1980s and 1990s and more recently for women bishops.

'When the campaign was taking place for women priests in the Anglican Church, I actually went and demonstrated with the women. And people said, "Are you an Anglican?" And I said, "No, but I just feel that if this shift happens here then it's more likely to happen in the Catholic Church as well." I just think it's important to have women in these institutions in roles where they can slowly make these changes. If you are able to get this through then in turn it will eventually happen in the Catholic Church as well, which I firmly believe.

'I campaigned with the women and occasionally wrote things because at that time I was doing a lot of work on women and the law. I had looked at the reasons that were given for keeping women out of the legal profession and indeed to keep them out of the medical profession and so on. And the same arguments that were used to keep women out of everything, the professions, politics and so forth were exactly the same kind of arguments in the Church. I know that they reach back and look at a literal interpretation of scripture but almost invariably it's the same kind of thing that somehow women are special and their place is special but it's over here and it doesn't involve being at the heart of the matter. It was interesting to draw to people's attention the parallels and the way in which the arguments are made and the way in which male-dominated institutions reach for the same arguments when it comes to excluding women. And sometimes it's by flattery and not just by saying that we're somehow not up to the game.

'And so I was keen to be involved in the campaign for women bishops. It always seemed bizarre to me that once that concession had been made [ordaining women as priests] then there would be this idea that you would be allowed in but you're not then allowed to reach the higher echelons. It just seemed a nonsense to me. And it's those backlashes that then take place, where people just cling on and fight every battle as though they're starting again. I think women will become bishops in the Anglican tradition and it's just a matter of time. The number of opponents is shrinking and I think it's a vital way of the Church developing. It's not about "equal opportunities", which sounds like working in the Civil Service or working in the corporate world. I really think this is about our humanity. When it comes to our spiritual lives why should it be that the only people who are able to play that role of priest and minister should be male? It just seems to be that it's about a denial of the great strengths that women bring to life.

'Of course there are the theological arguments and people will still say, "It wasn't Christ's intention and his apostles were men" and so on. And yet, if you look a bit more closely, you don't ever find Christ saying, "You men do this and you women do that." You actually find women very close to him in his ministry and he gives them important roles. So I just think that those are excuses and we have to move beyond it. But when I look at the Catholic Church and my own tradition let's remember that, as an example, the Catholic Church was pretty late in the day in coming to the view that slavery was an unacceptable thing. They weren't at the vanguard in that struggle. They took quite a long time in coming to the idea that capitalism was a positive thing and perhaps their reticence on some forms of capitalism are ones that I have sympathy for. But, you know, the idea that you needed to have business and that you moved on from very basic forms of markets to more sophisticated ones, it took the Catholic Church a long time to get there but they soon got there when they saw the direction of travel. They saw that they were going to pay the price for it, which is that people will not participate and will see the shortcomings of the institution.

'One of the things that's interesting about the debate on women bishops in the Anglican Church is that it has constitutional implications. Although some people don't like it, we do have an established Church and by virtue of that the established Church has a presence in the House of Lords. Is it acceptable that there should be parts of the House of Lords with constituents representing a particular interest like the Church that should be exclusively male? I think there's a question about that constitutionally. I think that to have bishops creating law for our nation and for them to be saying, "We refuse to have women amongst our number," creates a constitutional question which we should be pushing at rather hard.

'So often it's about holding on to power. And the disposition of power and how it's maintained is something that's very interesting to me, in all of my life, whether it's with regard to law or where I see it here in my work in the House of Lords. Power is about the ability to be able to effect change and to basically lead. And those who lead in the Catholic Church and who have the power to make decisions which affect the lives of everybody else are exclusively male. Until we have a real presence of women then my whole experience of law has been that until you bring in the female perspective then you're distorting your institution. And I think that you get dysfunction when you don't embrace all aspects of our humanity.

'It was very interesting, when we had the recent exposure of the Cardinal in Scotland [Cardinal Keith O'Brien retired after admitting to inappropriate sexual conduct with priests] and his public apology, I expressed a public view to a journalist that I felt compassion for him. I do feel compassion for him but I was criticised for that. I received a lot emails from people who said, "Why are you feeling compassion for him and not for his victims?" Well, of course, it goes without saying that I feel compassion for his victims. I've been a great champion of better protections for people who are exploited or abused all my professional life. But we also have to understand what it is that makes abusers and what it must be like to be someone who has to live a life in which they're having to bury their true sexuality and in which they have a high degree of self-loathing because they're told frequently that what they're being is an affront to the teachings of the Church which they've committed themselves to. I feel incredible compassion for people who have to live a lie and then have to find solace for their desires in behaviour that is inevitably exploitative or secretive or which carries a taint. But I think that's part of the Church's failure to really embrace the fact that as human beings we all have sexual needs and I think that gets the Church into lots of trouble.

'The Catholic Church is going to have to change. There are parts of the north of Scotland where there are no priests or there's a shortage of priests. And so the only answer is that they'll send somebody to give out Communion and they'll have women as sacramental ministers and it will be women who will be sitting at people's beds helping people at death and so on. But there's a shortage of priests so what are we going to do when communities want the Mass and don't just want somebody coming and giving out Communion and praying with them. That's not enough; Mass matters in the Catholic tradition and you need a priest for it. The idea that people should be waiting and not having their children baptised until there's some kind of grand tour when the priest will come in three months' time and just collect up all the babies at once is all wrong. People want their children baptised soon after they're born, as that's part of the Catholic tradition.

'And what about death? What about people wanting the

last rites? How are we going to deal with that? What you're going to find is that we've been sucking up the priests from the developing world, priests from Africa, India, Sri Lanka, the Philippines and so forth, when they should really be looking after their own people. It's almost like the NHS stealing nurses from poor countries. I think that a moment of decision will come. It will take a brave Pope but it will happen. And I thought it was very interesting that the new Pope Francis is surrounding himself with advisors who are not the insiders who have always run everything and so that in itself is a breakthrough. And it will be interesting to see whether this new Pope makes a difference. These things do take time, I know, and the pace is frustrating but it will happen and it will happen as an inevitability because the institution will not be able to function without women.

'It was a senior woman in the law who once said to me, "Don't rock the boat." And I thought about it hard and I thought, "Well you do have to but there are ways that you can do this." And I think, as I got older, I became better and more effective at doing it by both being reasonably brisk but also reasonably pragmatic, in that I don't think that things can happen right away but I do think you have to be persistent. I think that we, as women, mustn't allow ourselves to be readily bought off. We also have to remember that there are going to be women who say they don't want it, but there was a great posse of women who opposed women getting the vote. The same happened with changes in the law. There were some women who said, "It will come, it will just come as a matter of time, don't rock the boat." There were women who felt that we mustn't be strident about it, and there was a fear that if you were too noisy it would create a backlash and it wouldn't be collegiate and it's very important that the men like having us around.

'It was very funny because I had this experience recently where I was complaining about the fact that there had been three spaces all at once on the Supreme Court. We all thought, "Well they'll at least give one of them to another woman." And not a bit of it, they all went to nice, white men of a certain age. And the interesting thing you have to ask is who the gatekeepers are and what are the criteria for deciding that somebody's any good. If it's the fellows that are deciding on merit then sometimes the skills that women bring to things are not given a high score and you get the risk of cloning. So I said to one of these senior men, "23 people are consulted and 22 of them are men? Why didn't you have another woman?" And he said, "Oh, you know ... the right calibre is so important", blah blah. I mentioned a particular woman to him and he said, "Oh no, she's too pushy." And I just thought if it were a man you would think he was properly ambitious and he was keen to get onto the Supreme Court but if it's a woman you see that as unattractive.'

Helena is particularly well-known for her work on human rights and for standing up for women in very challenging situations such as those in violent relationships. Again this seemed to link to her upbringing in Glasgow and to the way her family understood their religion and politics to mean that you embraced the humanity of the other. She clearly felt that the behaviour of the Church has led to the marginalisation of women and at one point had chaired an enquiry into human trafficking. I wanted to know more about the kind of cases she had worked on and why she had remained so passionate about this kind of abuse of women.

'I've done lots of hard cases involving women *in extremis* and they're often Catholics, they're Catholics as much as they're anything else. Women who end up killing their partners because of being hideously abused over years, girls who get pregnant and then don't tell anybody for fear of what it will mean in their family and the reprisals. We think about some of the awful things that are taking place as happening in the new immigrant communities but it's not that long ago when girls were ostracised from communities here if they had an illegitimate baby. The line was that you were ruined for life and would never get yourself a decent husband if you were considered to have made the big mistake.

'I always remember, as a child, my mother holding my hand and taking me along the road to school and a women stopping my mother and saying to her, "Oh Mrs Kennedy, did you know that Mrs Coyle's daughter's got herself into trouble?" I could feel my little hand being squeezed tight by my mother because obviously my mother bristled. And my mother said, "Can I just say to you, I have nothing but sadness for Mrs Coyle and for her daughter. I've got four daughters of my own and I don't know what's in front of me so I'm not criticising anybody," and she dragged me off along the pavement. But it was that whole thing that people were so hypercritical of girls that had had sex before marriage. And it's just that that's the world now, and it's happening with the young Catholic couples like everybody else. Almost invariably they are going to try out sex before they're married and so the Church should just get real with it.

'I was involved in a particular case that I wrote about in the *Tablet* and mentioned in a talk that I gave about Lent and the issue of abandonment. It was about a little girl aged about 12 who was brought here by her immigrant family. They were living in Tower Hamlets and they sent for her from Bangladesh where she'd been living with her granny. I couldn't help but feel that they'd sent for her because they wanted somebody to be a skivvy, to look after the younger children that they'd had since coming, because that would be expected of a girl back home in rural villages.

'And she arrived and wasn't sent to school. She fell through the slats and was at home in this tower block looking after them all and she would be there during the day doing the cleaning and the washing when the mother would take the younger ones to school. And her mother's brother used to work in a tandoori restaurant and he would come home and he would be sleeping during the day because he'd be working most of the night and in the evenings. And he raped her, he had sex with her and the child became pregnant but didn't dare to tell anybody because she knew the implications of it. Nobody seemed to notice anything about this kid and she gave birth in the bathroom in the early hours of the morning while her parents and her siblings were asleep. She gave birth to this baby and in terror opened the bathroom window, having cut through the umbilical cord, and threw the baby out. The baby was found by people heading off to work around seven in the morning; somebody saw the baby and thought it was a doll. The baby survived with a fractured skull and was taken into care. Because of the trajectory police were able to work out where this baby was likely to have been thrown from and they went into the tower block and stopped different families. When they looked around the flat of this particular household there were signs of blood in the bathroom, in a bucket where she had put the trousers of her *salwar kameez*, and the parents hadn't even noticed. As she was being taken to the police station she started to deliver the placenta and it was only in the hospital when a young Bangladeshi doctor spoke with her that she told the story of how she had become pregnant.

'Well, you know, she was the person that was put on trial at the Old Bailey for the attempted murder of this baby. And yet here was a family that had not sent her to school and the brother of the mother disappeared into the ether and was hidden by other members of the community. Her mother and father were outraged and insisted that she must have had a secret boyfriend, covered up for the brother and didn't want her any more. She was now no longer marriageable or anything. It was the most horrific business. And the brother has still not been found, he's never been prosecuted. In the end I managed to persuade the Court to accept that it was an attempted infanticide. Infanticide was brought into being to stop women going to the gallows for destroying a newborn because almost invariably they were poor women who did it, *in extremis*, made pregnant by their masters. Or even if they were well-off girls, they were often girls who had been abused. And so juries didn't want to convict, and they created the new offence of infanticide. And we had some doubt as to whether attempted infanticide even existed because nobody had any experience of ever having had anyone charged with it before. But I got them to agree to place that in the indictment as well and we pleaded guilty to that and my memory is that she was given a conditional discharge.

'I remember telling the Judge the story about the family and about how this girl was now in care and that the baby was also in care, rejected. I was very worried about the future for that girl and the Judge was wonderful and said, "There's nothing that breaks your heart more in the law than seeing the wrong people in the dock when guilt really lies elsewhere." And when he sentenced her he said, "I'm giving you a conditional discharge and I want it to be clear that this is not a reflection on the value of your baby daughter's life and the fact that this terrible thing was done but it was as a result of what was done to you and there are people who bear greater responsibility."

'It just reminded you of why human rights are so important, the right of a child to an education, the right of a child not to be abused, sexually or otherwise and the responsibilities of parents and parenting. And that it's not good enough to say people have different traditions, there are some things about what it means to be human.

'Over the years I've probably done about six cases of girls killing babies, of women getting pregnant usually in that cusp of adolescence when people are in their teens and frightened to tell their families. The more strictly religious the family is, almost invariably the more likely it is that these things happen and class doesn't matter. I represented a girl from a very privileged background who gave birth, again at home, when her parents weren't there and put the newborn baby into her sports kit bag and when it started to move beat it with a hockey stick. Crazed out of her head that her parents were going to find out and punish her and unsure about what would happen to her, just desperate stuff. I find that strict adherence to rules that say that you are sinful if you are a sexual being is just, for me, unacceptable.

'When it comes to my own faith I always make it very clear that I think life is full of contradictions and people take spiritual sustenance in different ways. But it has to be possible for you to criticise institutions but at the same time know that some aspect of it fulfils some human need that we have. And I still love the business of a spiritual space and I think that those things are important to people. But I know lots of people who share my views about the horror of the Catholic Church's failure to engage adequately with what it means to be a sexual being and I think that the Church is screwed up by insisting on celibacy. Some people choose to be celibate and as people get older it becomes easier for them because that's the nature of ageing. But some people find that very, very hard and I think to make it a demand of someone that they can't be a priest and cannot minister to a community and be someone who assists someone in their relationship with the Almighty without being celibate is a requirement too far. And I think that it's locked into the whole business, of course, of protecting the institution's property. It was about the Church not wanting to pass on Church property

to wives and children and heirs and all of that. And I think
that it does present challenges about paying for it all. I can just
imagine that the Church will say, "Yes, let's have women priests
but they too have to be celibate," because they'll see it as being
a cheaper version, a cheaper way of doing it. Whereas providing
for a family, providing the kind of accommodation that a family
needs and so on, is a costly business.'

As she finished speaking I felt so grateful that there are people
like her who have the courage to stand up and fight injustice. I
deliberately chose to end this book with Helena. Although she
comes from a different Christian tradition than mine, her themes
are common to all Christian experience. She is right to say that
the issue of women in the Church is not about 'equal opportunities', although her experience is that similar arguments have
been used in all professions to hold women back and miss out
on the great gifts they bring. Instead it is about looking to the
example of Jesus and his treatment of women. He showed us
what it means to embrace all aspects of humanity if we are to
change the world for the better. There is no doubt in my mind
that a patriarchal Church has contributed to the marginalisation
and suffering of women all over the world. Can it be right to
keep women waiting any longer?

Favourite verse: 1Corinthians 13.1 'If I speak in the
*tongues of mortals and of angels, but do not have love, I
am a noisy gong or a clanging cymbal.'*

Favourite woman: Mary Magdalene. *I have known and
represented so many 'fallen' women and they are often the
most wonderful women. The resilience of women when
they've gone through so much is extraordinary because
very few women ever become prostitutes without having
an incredible back-story about the road that took them
there. And what the story of Mary Magdalene shows you
is the great compassion of Christ and that he sees what
is real and doesn't make easy judgements. I always liked
that sense of compassion and I don't think it is about
forgiveness because I don't think that he really saw her as
sinful.*

Glossary

Acolyte – a person assisting a priest in a religious ceremony.

Alpha Course – a series of interactive sessions that enable people to explore the basics of Christian faith.

Anglican Communion/Anglican Province – Anglicans trace their Christian roots back to the early Church and specifically to the post-Reformation expansion of the Church of England and other Episcopal Churches. The Anglican Communion has more than 80 million members in 34 provinces in 161 countries. The Churches are autonomous but linked by their relationship to the Archbishop of Canterbury. The celebration of Holy Communion is at the heart of Anglican worship.

Apostolic Succession – the teaching held by some Christians that bishops represent a direct, uninterrupted line of continuity from the apostles of Jesus Christ.

Archdeacon – a senior Church leader who often assists the more senior bishop with administrative and pastoral duties in a diocese.

Chalice and paten – the goblet and plate usually used during Communion.

Christian Unions – missional communities on student campuses across Britain.

Church Missionary Society (CMS) – an organisation that helps the world know more about Jesus.

Dean – usually the chief cleric in a cathedral or other collegiate church and head of a chapter of canons.

Diocesan and suffragan bishops – a diocesan bishop has charge of a specific diocese in the Anglican Church (43 in England), whereas a suffragan bishop is subordinate to them. Some suffragan bishops have been appointed to look after certain parishes that object to the ordination of women and are known as Provincial Episcopal visitors.

Ecclesiology – the study of the nature, constitution and functions of the Church.

Ecumenical – representing the whole Christian world (whether Roman Catholic, Protestant or other).

Episcopal Church – part of the worldwide Anglican Communion, largely based in the USA but with 110 dioceses in 16 nations (see Chapter 10). The Scottish Episcopal Church is also part of the Anglican Communion.

Eucharist – the Christian sacrament of Holy Communion.

Evangelist – someone who preaches the Christian gospel.

General Convention – the governing body of the Episcopal Church, including the House of Deputies and House of Bishops. It meets every three years in the USA and considers a wide range of important matters facing the Church.

General Synod – the highest governing body in the Church of England. It considers and approves legislation affecting the whole Church, debates key issues and approves the annual budget.

High Church – the term often used to describe Anglican churches that use a number of rituals associated with Roman Catholicism.

Liturgy – a particular form of public Christian worship.

Millennium Development Goals (MDGs) – eight MDGs were agreed on by world leaders at a UN summit in 2000. Targets were set to: eradicate extreme hunger; achieve universal primary education; promote gender equality; reduce child mortality; improve maternal health; combat HIV, AIDS, malaria and other diseases; ensure environmental sustainability; and develop a global partnership for development.

Patristics – the study of early Christian theolgians, such as Clement of Rome and Ignatius of Antioch.

Primate – a bishop who presides over a large region or entire nation.

Reception – the Christian understanding is the acceptance (or not) of a development in part of the Church by the whole Church.

Rochester Commission – set up following the General Synod of July 2000 to study theological and practical issues around the potential appointment of women bishops. Its report was published in 2004.

Systematic theology – a discipline of theology that attempts to provide a rational and coherent account of Christian faith and beliefs.

The Passion – the Passion of Christ refers to the short final period of Jesus' life covering his visit to Jerusalem, his arrest, trial, suffering and death by crucifixion on the cross.

Thomas Merton (1915–68) – an Anglo-American Catholic monk, writer and social activist.

Total Common Ministry – when all baptised members of a congregation minister together.

About the Author

Julia Ogilvy is a businesswoman, social entrepreneur and writer. She won a number of awards for her role as Managing Director of Hamilton & Inches, including Scottish Businesswoman of the Year. She is the founder and Honorary President of Project Scotland, a revolutionary national volunteering organisation for young people and won the Ernst & Young Scottish Social Entrepreneur of the Year Award. She was a member of the Prime Minister's Council for Social Action and on the board of Lloyds TSB Scotland. She is an elder in the Church of Scotland, a trustee of Tearfund, Buttle UK and a number of other organisations. Her first book was *Turning Points* and she is married with two children.

Please visit www.facebook.com/womeninwaiting for more information.

Note from the Author

If you have found it interesting to read about the work of the Christian international relief and development charity Tearfund (mentioned in the Introduction and Chapter 6) please do go to their website www.tearfund.org to find out more and consider giving a donation to help transform lives across the world. Tearfund is known for its ability to respond decisively when disasters strike around the world. It also mobilises powerful coalitions to advocate for political change on issues like corruption and climate change which particularly affect the poor. But central to their work is the mobilisation of the local church to live up to its Christian calling. Their ten-year vision is to see 50 million people released from material and spiritual poverty through a worldwide network of 100,000 local churches.

List of Illustrations

Chapter

1. Lucy Winkett © John Swannell
2. Sheila Watson © Jim Holden/Alamy
3. Rose Hudson-Wilkin – Reproduced with kind permission of contributor
4. Vivienne Faull – Reproduced with kind permission of the Chapter of York
5. Tamsin Merchant © Rob Merchant
6. Elaine Storkey © Clive Mear/Tearfund
7. Jane Williams © David Levenson/Getty Images
8. Sarah Coakley © Steve Bond
9. Alison Elliot © Photo Express
10. Katharine Jefferts Schori – Photo courtesy of Domestic and Foreign Missionary Society
11. Chilton Knudsen © Kara Flannery
12. Helena Kennedy – Reproduced with kind permission of contributor